HORSES and RIDERS

Volume 7

True Tales of the Old West

by

Charles L. Convis

Illustrated by Betsy McLeod
Cover by Mary Anne Convis

PIONEER PRESS, CARSON CITY, NEVADA

Manufactured in the United States of America

Library of Congress Catalog Card Number: 96-68502

ISBN 0-9651954-7-3 (Volume)
ISBN 0-9651954-0-6 (Series)

Printed by
KNI, Incorporated
Anaheim, California

CONTENTS

ILLUSTRATIONS

TWELVE THOUSAND MILES IN THE SADDLE

Juan Bautista Valdés deserves to be remembered. Unfortunately we have only large outlines, few details. He was a soldier in the army of New Spain when Gaspar de Portolá chose him to ride as courier with his 1769 expedition from San Diego, searching for Monterey Bay.

The explorers left San Diego in July, two days before Father Junípero Serra founded the first mission in the new land. They missed Monterey Bay in the coastal fog, but they continued north and discovered San Francisco Bay. Near starvation, they had to eat a dozen mules before they got back to San Diego in January, 1770.

Soon Portolá marched north again, this time finding Monterey Bay and starting a mission and presidio there. In June, 1770, he sent Valdés to Mexico City to report the founding of the two missions and the discovery of San Francisco Bay.

Viceroy Carlos de Croix sent Valdés back north with instructions to Pedro Fages, commandante of California, to explore San Francisco Bay for the purpose of establishing a presidio and mission there. The courier left with that message on November 12, 1770, reaching Monterey six months later.

Valdés was back in Mexico City in the summer of 1773. In late September he was sent north again on a 1500-mile ride to Tubac, south of present Tucson. This time he carried dispatches to Juan Baptista de Anza to search for an overland route between Sonora and the California coast. Valdés reached Tubac in early November.

The next January Valdés guided Anza's exploring expedition. He was selected for his knowledge of California roads and trails, gained while riding as courier with Portolá.

Anza's expedition looped down into Sonora and then back up to cross the Colorado River near present Yuma. They reached San Gabriel on March 22. On March 30 Anza sent a pack train of fifteen mules to San Diego for supplies. Valdés guided the train.

The pack train returned to San Gabriel on April 5. Two weeks later Anza sent the intrepid rider back to Mexico City with dispatches to the viceroy. In his diary of the expedition, Anza called Valdés the "extraordinary courier."

Two soldiers rode with Valdés to the Presidio of Altar, and one continued on with him to San Miguel de Horcasitas.

From there to Mexico City, almost a thousand miles, Valdés rode alone.

On all these trips Valdés rode through lands of hostile Indians who sometimes attacked intruders. Besides official dispatches to the viceroy, to local governors, and to other officials, Valdés carried the diaries kept in Anza's expedition, plus other letters. From these priceless sources, we can extract most of what we know about the early exploration of California.

Valdés galloped into Mexico City on June 14, 1774. Viceroy Antonio Bucareli was jubilant about Anza's success. He immediately ordered Valdés' testimony to be taken under oath to preserve details about Upper California.

In his deposition, taken the day of his arrival in Mexico City, Valdés provided extensive information about the topography and geography of California, the vegetation and wild life, and his estimates of distances between major points. It had been commonly thought that San Diego and San Gabriel were forty leagues apart and San Gabriel and Monterey sixty. Valdés thought, based on his experience in riding over the land, that these distances were more like sixty leagues and one hundred leagues. His estimates were remarkably close for the San Gabriel-Monterey distance and slightly exaggerated for the San Gabriel-San Diego distance.

Valdés had seen Father Junípero Serra in San Diego. He reported on the father's health and the condition of his frigate, *Nueva Galicia.* He also reported on Anza's plans to continue his expedition on to Monterey, and on the travels of Fathers Juan Díaz and Francisco Garcés, the two priests who accompanied Anza.

Valdés rode over three thousand miles with Portolá, including the reporting trip to Mexico City. He rode almost five thousand miles carrying the orders to Fages and returning to Mexico City. He rode almost four thousand miles with Anza, including the journey north from Mexico City and the return to report.

Herbert Bolton, leading historian of the Southwest, did not exaggerate when he said the extraordinary courier deserved to be remembered. It would be hard to put a price on what Juan Baptista Valdés' twelve thousand miles in the saddle meant to the exploration and settlement of California.

Suggested reading: Herbert E. Bolton, *Outpost of Empire* (New York: Alfred A. Knopf, 1931).

MUSTANG GRAY

Maberry B. Gray was seventeen when he came to Texas from South Carolina in 1835. Shortly after his arrival, he joined a buffalo hunting trip to no-man's country between the Nueces River and the Rio Grande, far to the southwest of the settlements.

While chasing buffaloes, Gray got separated from his companions. His horse fell, throwing him. He jumped to his feet, uninjured. But before he could grab the reins, the horse, excited by the chase, galloped away and out of sight.

Gray wandered on foot for hours, hoping in vain to find his horse or the other hunters. Darkness found him alone in a vast area of silence and solitude.

He rose at dawn after a night of thirst and worry to continue his search. He found a wounded buffalo in a thicket. He still had his rifle and ammunition, so he killed the animal. He cut off some meat and looked for water. He found a small pond where he drank, made a fire, and enjoyed his rude meal.

Gray saw horse tracks at the edge of the pond. Then he saw a band of wild mustangs galloping in his direction. He climbed a tree and watched them pass beneath to the pond. Some were fine looking animals. As they pawed the ground, drank, and whirled away, Gray wondered if he could capture one and ride it back to the settlements.

Gray returned to the buffalo carcass and skinned it with his Bowie knife. He trimmed the hide into a smooth oval and spent the day carving it into narrow strips, working from the outside in. He braided the strips into a long, leather rope, made pliable with buffalo fat. He cut the rope into a short length for a halter and a longer length for a lariat.

The next morning, as the time approached for the band to return for its morning drink, Gray tied one end of the lariat to a strong branch in the tree. Then he climbed the tree, holding the other end in a loop. He found a place where he could swing the loop without hitting branches, knowing that he would have only one chance to catch a horse. If he missed, they would not be back.

He did not miss. He roped a stout stallion. It lunged against the end of the rope, but the buffalo-skin lariat held. Gray climbed down as the rest of the herd galloped away.

The mustang reared, screamed, and plunged, but the lariat held fast. After the animal fell to the ground, exhausted and choking, Gray loosened the noose so the horse could breathe. He worked with the mustang a long time, getting him accustomed to the sight, smell, and touch of a man. He made a halter and slipped it over the mustang's head.

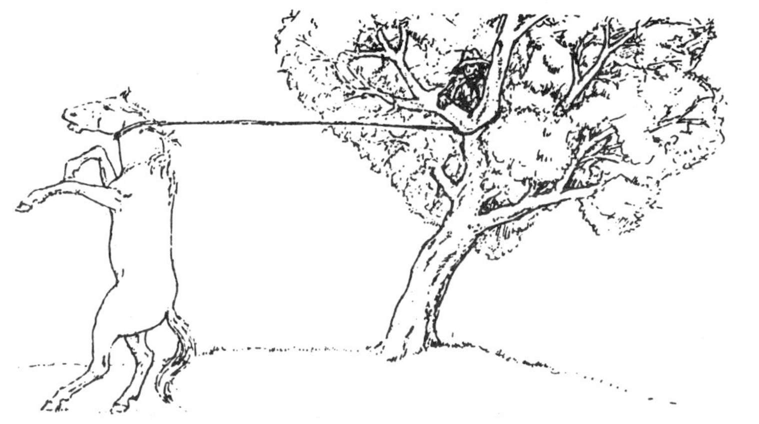

With the horse still tied to the tree limb, Gray jumped on its back. The stallion tore away, throwing Gray and jerking himself down when he hit the end of the rope. Gray continued working with the horse, talking to him, petting him, blowing his breath into the animal's nostrils. Finally, late in the day, Gray knew it was time for the big gamble.

He fastened his rifle to his back, untied the lariat, and jumped back on the mustang. He wondered if he could hold on to the lariat should the horse throw him again. The mustang leaped and bucked, but Gray steered him over the open prairie in the direction of the settements and hung on. He never found out whether he could hold the lariat if he got thrown off, because he stayed on. As the mustang tired, it ran smoother, bucked less.

When night came Gray hobbled the horse and staked it out. Away from its own range, the mustang grew to fear the rope and obey its new master. Gray had little difficulty mounting him the next morning.

They traveled several days and, quite by accident, came upon the camp of Gray's companions, who had given him up for lost. From that time on, he was always called Mustang Gray. By that name he lives in history, legend, and song.

The next spring Gray fought under General Houston at San Jacinto. He captained a company of Texas Rangers in the war against Mexico, and died in the arms of a sympathetic señorita in 1848. His body was returned to Texas and buried somewhere near Rio Grande City in an unmarked grave.

The Ballad of Mustang Gray has been sung in many ranger camps along the Texas border and in many cow camps along the Chisholm Trail.

Suggested reading: J. Frank Dobie, "Mustang Gray: Fact, Tradition, and Song," in *Tone the Bell Easy* (Austin: Texas Folk-Lore Soc. 1932).

MESSENGER OF DEATH

James Butler Bonham, 28-year-old lawyer, closed his Alabama office when he got the letter describing the "stirring times afoot" from his friend, William Barrett Travis in Texas. Travis wanted Bonham to come out and get in on the excitement.

Bonham didn't need encouragement. He came from a long line of rebels, people restless for adventure. He had been expelled from South Carolina College for what his classmates called devotion to freedom and the administration called insubordination.

Alabama women were sorry to see him leave. Disappointed in love, the six-foot two-inch, dark-eyed, wavy-haired bachelor had never married. He had been jailed once, when he thrashed a man in court for insulting his client, a lovely southern belle.

"You apologize to the court," the judge ordered.

"I should pull your nose, too, you old reprobate."

The judge gave him ninety days. Local women brought him food and flowers for his entire imprisonment.

Bonham, the son of wealthy South Carolina parents, was a skilled swordsman and an expert rider. He had heard that Texas horses, while not up to the thoroughbreds of the east, were surprisingly tough. Maybe he would get a chance to find out!

Shortly after Bonham reached Texas in December, 1835, he was commissioned a lieutenant in the Texas Cavalry. The next month General Sam Houston sent Bonham to San Antonio with Jim Bowie and thirty men. They carried orders to destroy the Alamo so Santa Anna's invading army could not use it.

Travis arrived with twenty-five men a few days after Bonham and Bowie rode in. Davey Crockett came with twelve more a few days after that. The officers promptly forgot Houston's orders. They would not blow up the Alamo! They would defend it!

Now Bonham was in his element! He organized a demonstration in San Antonio asking for more supplies, stating that "we cannot be driven from the post of honor."

But with six thousand enemy troops approaching, more men were essential. Colonel James Fannin had four hundred men just ninety-five miles away at Goliad. Someone should ride for help.

Bonham had often been called for courier duty during the two months he had been in Texas. Called on again, he saddled up and rode away to carry Travis's urgent request for help.

Fannin said, "no."

Bonham took his time riding back with the disappointing answer. But on February 23, not far from San Antonio, he heard the ominous boom of cannon and he knew the Alamo was under siege.

For the next four days, the defenders endured a continual bombardment, but casualties were few and morale remained high.

Travis, now commanding the post, had halted their return fire to conserve ammunition. How long could they hold out? Someone had to ask Fannin again for help. Bonham was the best choice. A superb horseman, he already knew the way.

"Tell Fannin he must come at once," Travis urged. "Tell him about the no-quarter flag flying on the church across the way. Without him, we haven't a chance."

"I'll tell him, Buck."

"We need to agree on a signal when you return, so we'll know it's you and can open the gate."

"I'll tie a white handkerchief around my hat."

"We'll watch. Good luck, Jim."

"I'll be back, Buck."

It took Bonham four days to reach Goliad and plead with Fannin for help. But Fannin had already tried to send half his men to San Antonio. He had to call them back. Fearing still another attack along the coast, he dared not deplete his garrison again.

Bonham turned back with his news of doom. When he reached San Antonio, he looked down on the Alamo from nearby heights. He could see the futility of trying to defend it against the massive army, clamoring at its gates. A fellow courier, safe outside the walls, said it would be foolhardy to throw his life away.

"Buck deserves to hear the answer from me," Bonham said. A faint grin showed on his face. "I told him I'd be back."

He tied a white handkerchief around his hat, patted his horse's neck and spurred forward. He plunged past the surprised Mexicans and through the open gate. He was the last man to enter the Alamo before Santa Anna's troops stormed over the walls, three days later.

James Butler Bonham had fought his last battle for freedom, justice, chivalry and honor. He was one of Texas' greatest heroes.

Suggested reading: Ben Procter, "James Butler Bonham," in *Heroes of Texas* (Waco: Texian Press, 1964).

HE RODE BETTER THAN A COMANCHE

In March, 1842, a delegation of Comanches came to San Antonio, seeking peace with the Texians. In honor of the occasion, Ranger Captain Jack Hays set up a riding match, where Comanches, the rangers, and Mexican rancheros would compete for prizes. He selected the prairie along San Pedro Creek, just west of San Antonio, for the contest. Most of the town, having heard stories about the riding skills of the contestants, came out to watch. A hundred fifty men competed for prizes of pistols, bowie knives, and Spanish blankets.

It was a colorful day. The rancheros wore high-crown, broad brim sombreros, with showy scarfs and slashed trousers. They held their fiery, gaudily-decorated mustangs in check with graceful pulls on the reins. Between forty and fifty Comanches, decked out in a savage finery of paints, feathers, and beads, looked on in traditional stoicism. Opposite them, drawn up in single file, their old Texas Ranger enemies, wearing buckskin with pistols and Bowie knives in their belts, galloped back and forth.

The match started with contestants snatching small objects from the ground while galloping at full speed. Hays himself could pick a half-dollar off the ground from a galloping horse, but that day a 17-year-old private in his company, John McMullin, would outride him. Next, the men shot pistols and arrows into targets, again while galloping at full speed. They fired from under the necks of their rushing mounts, hanging on to withers or a saddle horn with a heel or a knee.

The first matches finished with each contestant jumping from his horse at full gallop, running alongside for a few steps, then swinging under the horse's neck and up into the saddle on the other side. When these contests ended, McMullin was voted the most daring and graceful rider on the grounds. He was allowed to go first in the most exciting event of the day.

A wild horse which had never been ridden was snubbed to a post. McMullin blindfolded the animal and got a saddle on its

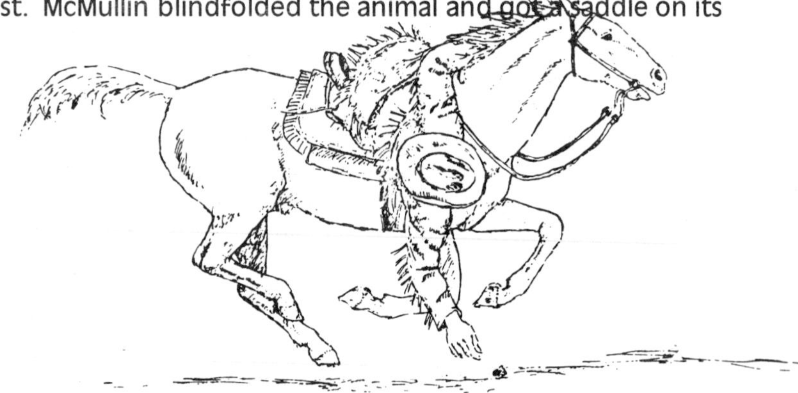

back and a bit into its mouth. Then he eased into the saddle, as the horse's quivering muscles showed the intensity of its terror. McMullin jerked the blindfold off, and the horse, screaming its rage, leaped forward and raced away. Instead of trying to check the animal, McMullin urged him on with quirt and spurs until he had completed a one-mile circle back to the cheering spectators. Then the horse bucked and plunged, trying vainly to throw its rider. Finally, it reared up and fell backwards.

Amid cries of horror from the crowd, McMullin calmly slipped out of the saddle and stepped aside. When the horse struggled to its feet, McMullin stepped back into the saddle. Then followed another dash and more bucking. When the young rider brought the horse back before the crowd in a slow canter, the black eyes of many señoritas admired the daring and handsome young ranger.

McMullin won first prize for horsemanship that day. Long Quirt, a Comanche, came in second.

About a year later, McMullin was one of 175 Texians captured by the Mexican Army at Mier. He survived the infamous Black Bean episode, when Mexicans executed every tenth prisoner. McMullin drew a white bean that day.

Released a year and a half later, most of the prisoners, including McMullin, returned to Texas to fight in the war against Mexico. By then a lieutenant, McMullin distinguished himself in the war. His company was the first to engage the enemy at Monterrey. He rode at a full gallop into a hail of bullets to scoop a wounded ranger off the ground

McMullin came to California in the gold rush. He raised horses in the San Joaquin Valley, near two of his close friends, Jack Hays, then the first elected sheriff of San Francisco, and David Terry, the supreme court judge who killed a United States senator in a duel.

At the beginning of the Civil War, McMullin was offered the overall command of the Texas Cavalry. He and his wife, the beautiful daughter of a famous Kentucky soldier and congressman, had four small children by then. The outstanding rider and brave warrior declined the post. He stayed home with his family.

Three years after the Civil War, by then with nine children and wealthy as a rancher, John McMullin, forty-four, died of typhoid fever. He is buried in Stockton's Rural Cemetery, across a narrow lane from his friend, David Terry, the dueling judge.

Suggested reading: Charles L. Convis, "John McMullin: Daring Texas Ranger, Wealthy California Rancher" in *San Joaquin Historian* (Stockton, Winter, 1993).

A LONG WINTER RIDE

Marcus Whitman had struggled to build the mission in the Oregon country. Henry Spalding, who had come out with him six years before, had another mission nearby, and Elkanah Walker had one near present Spokane. But church officials, unimpressed with the slow conversion of heathens, wanted to close the missions. Worse yet, the United States Government did not take Oregon seriously. Could they not see, thought Marcus, that the British, there first with their powerful Hudson's Bay Company, would take over? The new land needed more settlers from the states and a government interested in their future.

Now, in fall 1842, the settlers had begun coming. This last group even had two lawyers. Their companions teased them about being surrounded and almost captured by Indians at Independence Rock, but one of them, Amos L. Lovejoy, looked to Marcus like a man of substance. Maybe now Marcus should return to the states and lead more settlers out with wagons and families. Perhaps he could convince the government to move in ahead of the British. Perhaps Lovejoy would ride with him.

But no one had ridden across the mountains in winter. Both Indians and trappers knew enough to tent up for deep snows and raging blizzards.

"You cannot go," said Spalding.

"No man can survive on the open plains in winter," said Walker. "You will be lost."

"My first duty is to my country," Whitman replied. "This opportunity must not be lost."

Whitman, Lovejoy, and some Indian guides left Whitman's mission on October 3. Eleven days of hard riding brought them to Fort Hall on the Snake River near present Pocatello, Idaho. They had traveled over five hundred miles. Captain Richard Grant of the Hudson's Bay Company at Fort Hall tried to discourage them.

"It is a foolhardy journey," he said. "The snow in the mountains lies twenty feet deep already, and much more will come. The rivers are raging torrents. How can you survive?"

"God will protect us," Whitman insisted.

"The Sioux and the Pawnees, east of the mountains, are at war. They will kill you if you go that way."

"Then we'll turn south, through Spanish country."

Their guides returned to Oregon, so Grant gave them a new one.

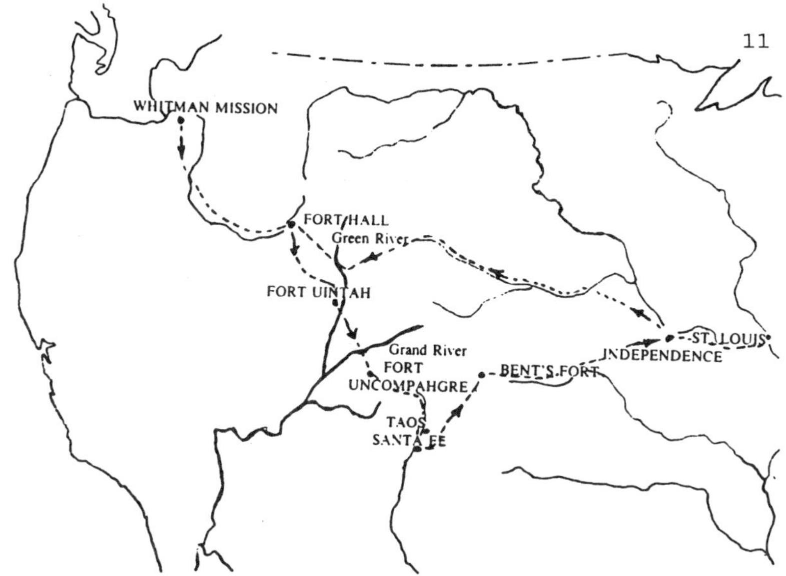

"An abandoned trail runs south from Fort Uintah," Grant said. "Mind you, if you do reach Santa Fe, you'll be the first white men to go that way. I fear greatly for your lives."

They headed southeast and reached Fort Uintah, without trouble. There they got a new guide who was sure he could lead them to Santa Fe.

Blizzards stormed over high ridges and through canyons, as they crossed from the Green River toward the Grand. They fed their horses on bark and heard wolves howl around their campfires. They took shelter for ten days in a deep ravine, but the storm still raged.

"We must ride on," Whitman said. "We must reach Washington before congress adjourns in early March."

They struggled out of the ravine, and the storm overwhelmed them. They wandered, lost, for hours. They tried to return to the ravine, but could not find their own tracks.

Finally Whitman knelt in the snow and prayed for guidance and protection, committing his little company, his wife, his mission, and his cause to God. As the missionary got back on his feet, the guide noticed the lead mule twitching his ears back and forth. Then the mule plunged into the snowdrifts.

"Look at the mule," the guide shouted. "He'll lead the way."

They followed the animal. In two hours they were back at their previous camp, blowing on the chilled embers of their morning fire. After the storm blew itself out, the guide refused to continue.

"I go back," he said. "I cannot take you further."

His pleas to the guide unheeded, Whitman rode back with him to Fort Uintah, and Lovejoy stayed with the animals. With only Whitman's faithful dog, Trapper, for company, Lovejoy waited a week in the deep snow. He kept busy cutting cottonwood twigs for the horses and logs for his fire.

Seven days later Whitman returned with another guide, and they resumed their journey. Their supplies had dwindled so much that they eventually had to eat a pack mule and Whitman's dog.

When they reached the Grand River they found ice reaching out two hundred feet from each bank, with a 200-foot freezing torrent roaring down the middle.

"It is impossible to cross," the new guide said. "I have never seen it this bad."

"We must cross, and now," Whitman insisted.

He dismounted and cut a cottonwood pole about eight feet long. Climbing back into the saddle, he put the pole on his shoulder and rode out on the ice. The horse sat back on his haunches, refusing to go forward.

"Now push us in," Whitman shouted.

Lovejoy and the guide skated the horse and its rider forward until they broke through and disappeared in the dark water. They surfaced several yards downstream. The horse swam until he found footing and then made for the far bank. Whitman helped his horse plow a channel through by using the pole to break ice. Then Whitman slipped out of the saddle, pulled the animal up on thicker ice, and led him to the bank.

Whitman collected wood for a big fire, while Lovejoy and the guide forced the rest of the animals into the river. Grasping tails, they safely crossed the ice-filled channel.

They followed the Gunnison River to Fort Uncompahgre, where they traded for fresh horses. They followed the Rio Grande through Taos and stopped in Santa Fe for more supplies, fresh horses, and news from the states. They rode on for Bent's Fort.

Water was now as scarce as wood. The bitter cold and deep snow had made big gray wolves a menace. One night Whitman split his axe handle cutting firewood. He wrapped the handle with rawhide and left the axe under the edge of his tent. The next morning the axe was gone, stolen by a hungry wolf. Whitman and Lovejoy shuddered to think what losing the tool would have meant earlier.

Shortly before reaching Bent's Fort, they met George Bent, leading a pack train to El Paso. Bent said a party of fifty mountain men were leaving the fort for St. Louis in two days, and there would not be another party going out until spring.

"I'll take two days' provisions and catch them," Whitman told Lovejoy. "You and the guide can stay at the fort until spring and then come on to the Missouri border. I'll meet you there on my way back to Oregon."

When Lovejoy reached the fort, he learned that Whitman had not been seen. Runners went out to stop the mountain men, and scouts started searching for Whitman. Lovejoy and a scout found an Indian who said he had discovered Whitman, lost, and had given him directions. That evening a cold, hungry Whitman walked into the fort. The next morning he mounted a fresh horse and hurried to catch up with the mountain men.

On a cold February morning, Marcus Whitman walked down the streets of St. Louis. Old mountain men, wintering in the city, begged him to tell how he had made such an impossible ride.

"I don't have time," he said. "I must get on to Washington."

Soon Whitman stood before President John Tyler. His ragged buffalo coat and worn leggings and moccasins were silent witnesses of his heroic ride. His eyes glowed as he told his dream for the nation's destiny.

By May, Whitman was back on the frontier, where he met his trail partner, Lovejoy. They led a thousand emigrants to Oregon in the great migration of 1843. They proved that large numbers of wagons with families could cross the mountains. Following in the wagon train's wake, John Charles Fremont — called the Great Pathfinder — led his first trip to the west coast.

President James Polk, who succeeded Tyler, said our country could thank Marcus Whitman that the territory northwest of the Rocky Mountains — Washington, Oregon, Idaho and parts of Montana and Wyoming — belonged to it and not to England.

Whitman had made a 3000-mile, monumental ride from Oregon to St. Louis, one of the most memorable journeys in our nation's history. The ride back was easy.

Suggested reading: O. W. Nixon, *Whitman's Ride Through Savage Lands* (Chicago: Winona Publishing Co., 1905).

CALIFORNIA'S PAUL REVERE

Slender John Brown, called Juan Flaco (Lean John), was born in Sweden. He enlisted in the Swedish Navy at fifteen. Then he joined Simon Bolivar's South American army of liberation. Taken prisoner, he escaped and fled to Southern California in 1828. He supported Juan Alvarado's 1836 attempted revolution, but a decade later he helped Governor Micheltorena put down another revolutionary attempt by Alvarado.

Juan supported the American conquest in 1846, proudly saying he was a Swedish native who had become a true American. When Marine Captain Archibald Gillespie claimed control of Southern California, Juan enlisted in his fifty-man company of volunteers.

But Gillespie's harsh curfews alienated the Angelenos, who shrugged their shoulders and watched six hundred well-armed Mexican soldiers surround the half-disciplined and poorly-supplied American troops. The nearest American reinforcements were four hundred miles away in Monterey. Jose Flores, the Mexican commander, demanded Gillespie's surrender. Gillespie asked for a volunteer to ride for help. Fifty-year-old Juan Flaco stepped forward.

Juan slipped out at sunset on September 25. Fifteen yelling, Mexican soldiers took up the chase. After a two-mile gallop, Juan's horse slowed for a thirteen-foot gully. The Mexicans fired their rifles, and a bullet zipped through the horse. He leaped the gully and struggled two more miles before falling dead. But the Mexican horses behind him had refused to jump. Juan continued on foot. By dawn he had traveled twenty-seven miles, more than the total ride of Paul Revere.

As the sky lightened in the east, Juan reached the Ranch of the Virgin owned by Domingo Dominguez. Juan did not trust Domingo, a loyal Mexican. He told Domingo that he was chasing a Frenchman, who had robbed him.

"I lost my horse when I stepped off to tighten the cinch," Juan said. "A grizzly spooked him."

Domingo gave Juan breakfast, a fresh horse, and a saddle. Tom Lewis of Boston, visiting the Dominguez ranch, joined Juan and they rode on.

At eleven that evening the riders reached the Presidio at Santa Barbara. Juan had spurred his horse so hard, the animal's intestines poked out through his hide. Juan and Lewis camped until dawn and then hailed Captain Talbot and his garrison of fifteen men. After Talbot gave them fresh horses, Juan and Lewis galloped away. They got four more fresh horses at the ranch of Captain Robbins, an American.

Twenty-five Mexicans thundered into Robbins' ranch fifteen minutes after Juan and Lewis left. They demanded fresh horses to continue their pursuit. Robbins said all he had were some run-down animals left by Fremont a few days before. Juan saw the sunlight glinting on the Mexicans' lances as he and Lewis climbed the ridge toward Santa Inez. By late evening they had reached the Arroyo Hondo, a ranch owned by another American named Burton.

After a short rest, they rode on with fresh horses, reaching a camp near San Luis Obispo the next evening.

"I'm beat," Lewis said. "Can't go a mile further."

Juan left him two horses and twenty dollars, and he struggled on.

The next night, September 29, Juan reached the Presidio at Monterey, commanded by Captain Maddox. He was too exhausted to eat. Maddox told him they would have to get the message for help to Commander Robert Stockton in San Francisco. He had no one else he could trust to make the ride.

The next morning Juan took a cold bath to force the soreness from his muscles. Maddox gave him the fastest animal in Monterey, a race horse owned by a Mister Dye.

Juan changed horses at the Angel Castro ranch, at Antonio German's ranch, and at the Ojo de Cocho. He reached the San Jose Puebla at noon. In his own words from his Navy days, he was "fluking" when he passed Santa Clara. He reached San Francisco at eight that evening. Juan slept on the beach and met the market boat from the U. S. frigate Congress the next morning, October 1. He boarded the vessel and reported to Commander Stockton.

Juan Flaco had traveled 350 miles to Monterey in four days. He had ridden 180 more miles the last day, at an average speed of twenty-two miles an hour. As incredible as the ride was, it was too late. The night Juan spent in Monterey, Gillespie was surrendering his forces in Los Angeles. Stockton did order additional troops to the south, however, and they eventually defeated the Mexicans.

Suggested reading: *San Joaquin Republican*, May 12, 1858, December 13, 1859 (Stockton, California).

EPIC RIDE FOR NOTHING

When John C. Fremont rode out of Cuidad de Los Angeles that March 22 morning in 1847, he had a good man on each side of him. Jacob Dodson, 24-year-old free black servant, had traveled with Fremont on his two expeditions to California. Don Jose de Jesus Pico had been taken prisoner when Fremont led his California Battalion south to help Commodore Robert Stockton and General Stephen Watts Kearny capture California. Condemned to death by court martial, Pico won a pardon from Fremont, and became a trusted aide and trail companion.

Two months before the ride, Fremont had accepted the surrender of rebellious Californios led by Don Jose's cousin, Don Andres Pico. Then he got caught in the Stockton-Kearny struggle for power. Each officer interpreted his orders from the president as authority to appoint California's first governor. Fremont sided with Stockton. He had Stockton's commission as governor in his pocket. He also had a new promotion from the president. So it was Lieutenant Colonel Fremont who rode north to warn Kearny at Monterey that the Californios planned a new rebellion! The Americans needed reinforcements at once!

The riders loose-herded six horses ahead as they galloped along the El Camino Real, the trail of the California Missions. Twenty miles out of Los Angeles, Dodson and Pico roped three fresh horses from the remuda. After a quick move of saddles and bridles, the riders thundered on up the San Fernando Valley.

They passed the San Fernando Mission and switched horses after another twenty miles. They climbed to a notch in the mountains and dropped down to the Santa Clara River.

"We'll eat here," Fremont said. "I figure we've gone sixty miles. Should reach Santa Barbara by evening."

Dodson built a fire and Don Jose sat down by the man who had saved his life.

"For you every day is too short, is it not so, señor?"

"Seems so, sometimes."

They saddled fresh horses and blazed through Mission Buenaventura. They reached the mission at Santa Barbara before nightfall. One hundred twenty miles the first day! Three hundred still to go!

Fremont, thirty-four and tough as rawhide, seemed short on the ground but tall in the saddle. With the consuming joy known to ambitious men on life or death missions, he looked forward to the remainder of the ride. But would Kearney believe the message from Stockton's supporter? He could only gallop on north and find out.

"Mucho mountains tomorrow, señor," Don Jose said.

"I know."

The second day was harder. Swinging away from the coast, they rode through mountains all day. They crossed the Santa Barbara and Santa Inez Ranges and rushed through the Santa Inez and La Purisima Missions. They stopped a few minutes at Captain Dana Goodwin's ranch, near the Santa Maria River. It was dark, but they still had three hours of hard riding to reach Mission San Luis Obispo.

By starlight they galloped along a narrow shelf, carved into the mountains which loomed up from the sea. They heard the pounding surf below as they raced onward. They reached the mission at nine. They had ridden 135 miles that second day! When Don Jose stood beside Fremont in the mission plaza that evening, his thoughts reached back a few months, to when he had faced the firing squad in the same plaza. He remembered Fremont's words of pardon.

"My friend," Pico said softly, "I will never forget."

After a sound sleep, the riders rushed on with a remuda of fresh horses. They crossed

Cuesta Pass and pounded along the foothills of the Santa Lucia Range. They passed the ruins of San Miguel Mission and crossed the Nacimiento and San Antonio Rivers. They only made seventy miles that day. They bedded down in the chaparral and willows of the Salinas Valley.

Back in the saddle at daybreak, they raced through San Antonio and Soledad Missions and saw the red roofs of Monterey in late afternoon. They galloped to the presidio, where the American flag waved in the on-shore breeze. They had covered 420 miles in seventy-six hours of riding.

But next morning, when Fremont was allowed to report to Kearny, the general paid no attention to the message about a rebellion. Instead he demanded that Fremont turn over all his public documents.

"My documents are in Los Angeles, general," Fremont said. "I don't take orders from you. My appointment as governor came from Commodore Stockton."

"Stockton has been replaced. He is gone from California." Kearny's words dripped with scorn. "You call yourself an officer? You present yourself to me dirty, out of uniform, and looking like you have slept in those rags for a week."

"But what about the insurrection? We must have reinforcements!"

Kearny was unmoved. Fremont and his companions galloped back to Los Angeles. This time fury motivated Fremont, and they raced back in four more days. Over eight hundred miles in eight days of riding!

A few weeks later, Kearny's men took Fremont to Washington, a virtual prisoner of war. He was court martialed and found guilty of insubordination. The president intervened, offering to re-instate Fremont's commission without any punishment. Fremont refused the offer and resigned from the army.

The second California rebellion never amounted to much. Some thought it existed only in Fremont's imagination, but it did produce an epic ride.

Suggested reading: Dabney Collins, *Great Western Rides* (Denver: Sage Books, 1961).

A QUICK TRIP ON THE SANTA FE TRAIL

François Xavier Aubry, twenty-four, was five feet two and weighed a hundred pounds. They called him "Little Aubry," but he was full of grit. A quiet man to know, he loved and chased adventure all his short life.

The little French-Canadian, raised in poverty in Quebec, had come to St. Louis at eighteen to clerk in a big store. But his concentrated energy demanded more then selling merchandise indoors. He soon struck it rich freighting on the Santa Fe Trail.

In September, 1848, Aubry was in Santa Fe after bringing his second wagon train out for the season. The stores were bare, and the town was full of volunteer soldiers, discharged from the Mexican War. If he could bring out a third train, Aubry could sell its cargo for top prices. He would have to ride back to Missouri quickly to get the train out ahead of winter snows.

Aubry had already ridden twice from Santa Fe to Independence that year. The first trip back had taken fourteen days, less than half the schedule for military mail. Five men who started with him had dropped out. Delayed by robbers, Indians, and January blizzards, he had covered the last three hundred miles in three days. Missouri newspapers said the ride was unprecedented on the plains. Aubry then decided to take a second train out to Santa Fe. No one had done that before. The Santa Fe freighters could not return their ox-teams to the states in time for a second trip.

"I'll get new oxen and bullwhackers back in Missouri," the determined Aubry said.

Aubry had bet that he could make the second trip in eight days. He won the bet, killing three horses and two mules on that ride. When he led his second train into Santa Fe in September, the town was still talking about his eight-day ride to Independence.

Now Aubry said he could ride back in six days! He put a thousand dollars behind his words. He had already arranged for relay horses at selected points along the trail. His bets were quickly covered — no one believed that a man could ride eight hundred miles in six days. Six men had started with him on the second trip. They had all fallen behind. Now he would ride by himself, a lone rider across an empty land.

Aubry leaped into the saddle before dawn on September 12 and galloped out of Santa Fe. He burned the

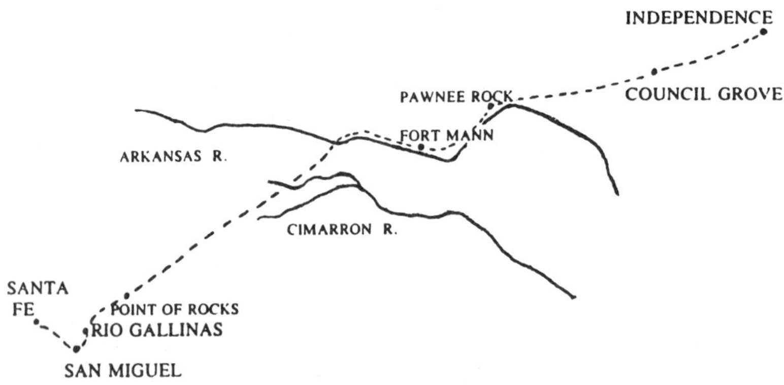

wind through San Miguel and on to Rio Gallinas (present Las Vegas), where three fresh horses waited. Riding one and leading the two spares, Aubry turned north and rode all night, sleeping and eating in the saddle. He strapped himself in, so he could doze without falling. He stopped only at relay points to change horses. Nearing Point of Rocks, he picked up his favorite horse, a dun-colored Spanish mare he called Dolly.

When he reached the next relay point, Aubry found no horses. His helper, left there to watch the horses, lay dead and scalped. Aubry spurred Dolly on. After riding the game little mare for two hundred miles in twenty-six hours, he met a wagon train and bought a fresh horse.

"You be sure and leave Dolly for me at a stable in Santa Fe," he cautioned the wagonmaster.

"I'll be sure. She's some horse ain't she?"

"Best I ever saw."

Aubry found three fresh horses where they had been left for him in some timber near the Cimarron River. But he pushed them too hard as he approached the half-way point. The first two horses gave out, and the third fell dead. He only got thirty miles out of the three.

Aubry hid his saddle and set out on foot, the bridle in his hand. In twenty miles he reached the Arkansas River at a place now called Aubry's Crossing. He staggered on to Fort Mann, near present Dodge City. There he borrowed a horse and saddle from a buffalo-hunter friend. He got fresh horses at Pawnee Rock and Council Grove. He covered the last hundred fifty miles at a swinging gallop, tied fast into the saddle.

Aubry had eaten only six meals on the ground, and had stopped only once for sleep — just two hours at that. He had ridden six horses to their deaths and had broken down six others. For one entire day and night, rain had fallen constantly. Streams were swimming deep.

Aubry made the ride in five days, sixteen hours. He won his bet with eight hours to spare. The exhausted man was lifted out of his bloody saddle and carried into the Noland House Hotel. He could barely whisper as he ordered something to eat.

The six-day ride was so spectacular no one ever tried to match it. Buffalo Bill Cody, who himself would make some famous rides with the Pony Express, said Aubry's ride was superhuman.

Aubry freighted three more years, growing wealthier each year. In 1852 he followed the gold rush to California, again riding Dolly, his little Spanish mare. The next year he drove fourteen thousand sheep to California. Indians attacked west of the Little Colorado River in Arizona, wounding both Dolly and Aubry. Two weeks later Aubry's men were suffering from near starvation and thirst when Dolly died. Recovering from eight wounds of his own, a grieving Aubry wrote in his diary:

"I have the misfortune to know that the flesh we are eating is that of my inestimable mare Dolly, who has so often saved me from death at the hands of Indians."

Aubry returned to Santa Fe in 1854, crossing over the mountains and desert by a new route which he had picked out. The route was later followed by the Santa Fe Railroad.

Aubry, thirty, was stabbed to death in the barroom of the La Fonda Hotel in Santa Fe in August, 1854. His assailant, Richard H. Weightman, a man of unsound mind, was acquitted. The jury said he acted in self defense. Aubry's name has been given to an army fort, a Missouri River steamship, and mountains and streets across the west.

Aubry's ride and Dolly's part in it have never been equalled by horse or man.

Suggested reading: Donald Chaput, *François X. Aubry, Trader, Trailmaker, and Voyageur in the Southwest, 1846-1854* (Glendale: Arthur Clark Co., 1975).

WILLIAM MANLY'S ONE-EYED MULE

William Manly and John Rogers reached Mission San Fernando in early 1850, after walking two hundred miles from Death Valley. They needed food and horses to return immediately to the eleven adults and four children, left behind in the desert. They had nearly starved reaching the mission, and they feared some of those left behind would starve before they could get back. They bought three horses, loading two of them with food. They would take turns riding the third.

A day or two later they overtook a man leading a skinny little one-eyed mule.

"Want to sell your mule?" Manly asked.

"She ain't much to look at," the owner said. "I got her when she was almost dead. She's comin' back slow. How much you figure to pay?"

"She looks like a skeleton, and there's that big sore on her back. How about fifteen dollars?"

"I reckon that's fair."

Manly moved the packs from one of their horses to the frail back of the little mule, mounted the horse, and they moved on at a faster pace. Manly became one of California's greatest heroes. The mule turned out as enduring as its new master.

With water holes thirty or more miles apart and often too salty to drink from, one of the horses soon died. The little mule was smarter and livelier than her trail companions. She cropped every spear of grass and every sagebrush leaf she could find along the trail. The horses grew weaker, and the men had to cache the wheat they carried, hoping to find it when they returned with the survivors.

After traveling about a hundred miles, Manly chose a short cut over some high mountains. It would save time, desperately needed to reach the stranded emigrants. But the mountains were too rough for the horses, and they had to be left behind. The piteous cries of the abandoned animals saddened the hearts of Manly and Rogers. They struggled on with the game little mule.

After going two days without water, the men came to a perpendicular wall about ten feet high. They could crawl up but it looked hopeless for the mule. Yet, the little animal had seemed so cheerful in bounding from rock to rock to reach the obstruction, they decided to give it a try. They piled loose rocks against the wall until they had made a slippery passageway, fifteen feet long and four inches wide at the top. Manly couldn't believe the little mule could do it, but she seemed willing to try. They tied all their ropes together and fastened them to the animal. With Manly in front and Rogers behind, they hoped they could help the little mule keep her balance.

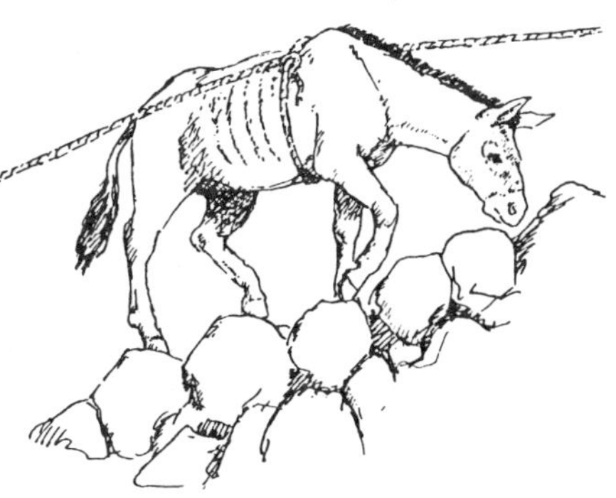

"Carefully and steadily she went along, selecting a place before putting down a foot, and when she came to the narrow ledge she leaned gently on the rope, never making a sudden start or jump, but, cautiously as a cat, she moved slowly along. There was now no turning back for her. She must cross this narrow place over which I had to creep on hands and knees, or be dashed down fifty feet to a certain death. When the worst place was reached she stopped and hesitated, looking back as well as she could."

Rogers wanted to yell at the animal and frighten her across. Manly said, "no" and continued to talk gently to the little mule. It was a time, Manly said, when the lives of the stranded 49'ers hung in the balance. Without the mule, they could not carry back the necessary food that the others would need.

"I gently pulled the rope, calling the little animal to make a trial. She smelled all around and looked over every inch of the strong ledge, then took one careful step after another over the dangerous place. She crept along, trusting to the rope for balance, till she was half way across. Then another step or two when, calculating the distance closely, she made a spring and landed on a smooth bit of sloping rock below that led up to the highest crest of the precipice, and climbed to the top, safe and sound above the falls."

Manly and Rogers lifted the pack of food up with the rope, loaded it back on the mule and continued on their way. All the emigrants got out safely. Later that year Manly went back to Wisconsin for a visit. He sold the courageous animal, by then a "fat little mule," to a friend.

Suggested reading: William Lewis Manly, *Death Valley in '49* (Los Angeles: Borden Publishing Co., 1949).

RACING A STEAMER

California cattleman Louis Remme deposited the $12,500 with Adams & Company in Sacramento. With the proceeds from successful cattle sales safely in the bank, he strolled into Bremond's restaurant for a leisurely breakfast. Proprietor Marius Bremond greeted his guest and handed him the morning paper, which had just come from San Francisco on that morning's riverboat.

Remme's smile slowly disappeared as he read the news of bank failures that February day in 1855. Then he heard excited chatter from other guests — "Page Bacon's cleaned out." "Adams, too." "Looks bad." Remme's face turned grim, and he shoved the menu away.

He leaped to his feet and ran back to the Adams office. He shouldered his way through the gathering crowd and pounded on the counter inside.

"I just made a deposit! I want my gold back, right now. Here's my certificate." He thrust it forward.

"Sir, you'll have to see the receiver," the cashier said. "You can get in line if you want. It looks like a long wait. There's nothing I can do." He shrugged and turned away.

Remme's brain whirled. Perhaps he could dash up to Marysville and get the gold there. Then he realized that the news from San Francisco would get there ahead of him. How about Grass Valley? Georgetown? Placerville? But the news would have arrived ahead of him at all those places. The savings of five years work! What could he do? Then it hit him — Portland!

Surely Adams had a branch in that distant city, almost seven hundred miles away. It had no railroad, no telegraph. The news would have to come by steamer from San Francisco — the same steamer that had just brought the news to California. The steamer would be sailing the next morning. Should he go down to San Francisco and take it?

But what's the good in arriving at the same time as the news? he wondered. Remme could imagine other milling crowds of determined depositors, demanding their funds, the sheriff' notices, the closed doors. His only chance was to beat the steamer to Portland!

Just then Remme saw a stern-wheeled river paddler leaving for Knight's Landing, forty-two miles up the Sacramento River. Remme decided instantly. He raced to the boat and jumped as the gangplank was being pulled in. He landed safely, ignoring the stares of the other passengers.

He got a horse from Knight, himself, when the boat landed. He galloped to the head of Grand Island and traded for a fresh horse from an old friend, Judge Diefendorf. He galloped on north, his face firm as he thought about the long ride ahead. And the steamer would travel day and night. Could he possibly beat it?

He bought and borrowed horses from friends and strangers up the Sacramento Valley and continued his race. Opposite the Sutter Buttes by sunset, he was in Red Bluff by ten. Five minutes later, a sandwich in his hand and a fresh horse between his knees, he galloped on.

Twenty miles further, he saw a campfire along Cottonwood Creek.

"Who's there?"

"Remme. A stockman. I'm after a thief. Need a fresh horse."

"Take this one. Good hunting!"

He began climbing as he left the flat Sacramento Valley behind. No longer would he average ten miles an hour. He struggled on to Shasta City and Whiskeytown. At dawn he stopped for breakfast at Tower House on Clear Creek. Old Bally Mountain loomed up to the southwest, its pink granite showing above dense cedar and pine. The going would be slower now with no more wagon trails until he reached Oregon.

All that day Remme climbed and circled around bluffs and headlands. The early spring of the Sacramento Valley was only a warm memory as he faced bitter winds and whirling snow, blowing down from the Trinity Mountains. He reached Trinity Creek after dark.

Money could not buy a horse, but a friendly miner loaned him one and gave him supper.

"Bring that thief back on my horse,

and I'll help you hang him."

Remme reached Scott Valley before daylight. He lay down, exhausted, and slept until noon. The soaring dome of Mount Shasta loomed up in the east as he leaped back into the saddle.

The traveling was easier past Callahan's, and he found wagon roads to follow. He heard cheers in Yreka, where he had a quick drink of brandy and borrowed a fresh horse.

He crossed the Klamath River and followed the long rise to Oregon. When he passed the cairn on the state boundary, he said to himself, "Thank God for Oregon."

Remme rode carefully between the Klamath and Rogue rivers, as the Modoc Indians were on the warpath. He galloped down the cold valley of Bear Creek and stopped for coffee and a two-hour nap in Jacksonville.

He crossed the Rogue River on a ferry, glad that he had seen no Indians in the Modoc country. But a few hours later, as he was walking his horse, he heard six rifles fire and a bullet whiz past his ear. He leaped onto his horse, dug in his spurs and outraced the Indians. When he reached Cow Creek, he pulled his horse back to a walk.

Remme enjoyed the beautiful Round Prairie, as he rode on to Winchester on the North Fork of the Umpqua. He stopped and rested at a tavern. He had five hundred miles behind him, two hundred to go! He kept wondering, Would he beat the steamer?

Remme ran into heavy rain in the pretty Yoncalla Valley. But he had outridden blizzards and Indians. The Oregon rain was no problem. He stopped at Jesse Applegate's cabin and got a fresh horse. He heard mountain lions howling in the forest as he rode on.

He reached the tiny city of Eugene just before daybreak. He bought a horse for seventy dollars, getting credit for sixty-five dollars for the one he left. He crossed the rain-swollen Willamette at Peoria. The day had turned off mild and clear. The Cascades loomed up in the east against a beautiful, blue sky. Remme thought of Mount Shasta, far behind. This was the fifth day of his ride. So far, he had had just ten hours sleep.

He rode the rest of the day and all night. He got a fresh horse for five dollars at breakfast. By ten-thirty he was in Oregon City and at noon in Milwaukee. There he crossed back over the rain-swollen Willamette. By one o'clock he was in Portland, after six days of riding.

As soon as he had his horse put up in a stable, he inquired about the steamer.

"Is the steamer in from 'Frisco, yet?" he asked.

"Not yet, but she's due in this afternoon."

"Where is Adams and Company?" Remme's voice was filled with relief.

The Adams agent was taking down the shutters after returning from lunch. A mud-spattered Remme approached him.

"Can you cash a certificate of deposit on your Sacramento office?"

"Regular charge is one-half of one percent for every thing over a thousand dollars. How much you got?"

"Twelve thousand five hundred. I'm a cattle buyer and I need the money."

The agent examined the certificate.

"It looks in good order, sir," he said, chuckling at the easy profit of $62.50. He set out ten stacks of gold slugs.

Remme stuffed the gold into his pockets, and said, "Thank you, sir," with a big smile. He hurried to his hotel. When the gold was safely locked in the hotel safe, he walked back to the street. He heard the cannon shot announcing the arrival of the steamer.

Before the lines were fastened ashore, the purser, Ralph Meade, leaped over the rail and ran to the Adams office. He got the $950 he had on deposit there, but no other depositor collected a cent.

Remme, smiling broadly through the fatigue of his long ride, was no longer a depositor. He had ridden 665 miles in 147 hours, ten of which went to sleep. He had averaged five miles an hour through rains, storms, Indians, and mud in his epic ride. His gold was safe!

Suggested reading: Neill C. Wilson, *Treasure Express* (New York: The MacMillan Co., 1936).

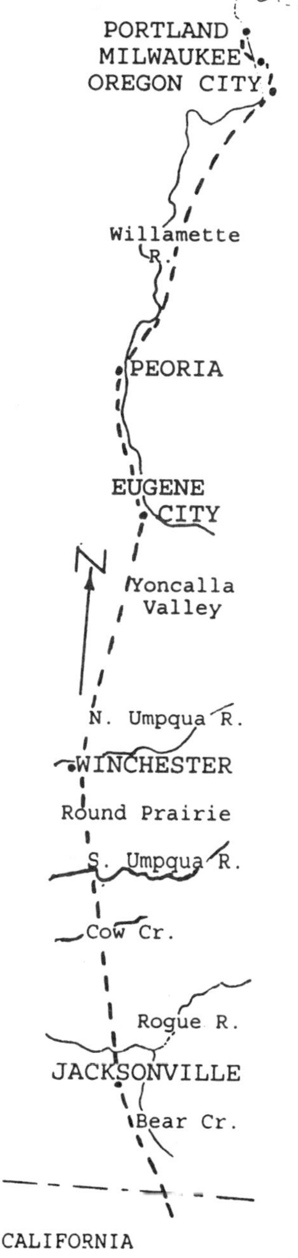

LOUIS REMME IN THE TRINITY MOUNTAINS

PONY BOB HASLAM

RIDING INTO THE CARSON VALLEY

PONY BOB'S RIDE

Robert "Pony Bob" Haslam grabbed the eastbound mochila and slapped it over his saddle. The Pony Express, just a few weeks old in 1860, was trying to carry mail between St. Joseph and San Francisco in ten days, as promised. Pony Bob was one of the "wiry fellows — not over eighteen — willing to risk death daily — orphans preferred" hired to ride from seventy-five to one hundred miles on each run, changing horses every twelve miles or so.

Pony Bob leaped into the saddle at Friday's Station on the south tip of Lake Bigler (Tahoe) and whipped his horse over the ridge toward his first relay stop at Genoa, Nevada. He shoved the whip under his leg and gripped the saddle horn tightly to stay seated as his horse lurched and slid toward the Carson Valley far below.

The afternoon sun was high in the May sky when the station keeper at Genoa helped switch the mochila, with its four pockets containing letters, to a fresh horse. The animal snorted, anxious to gallop away.

"Hear the Paiutes are on the warpath somewhere's down the line," the keeper said.

"I know what it feels like to get hit by Injun arrows," Bob said. "I'll watch careful."

Bob galloped on to Carson. "Keep an eye out for the redskins," the station keeper there warned. "I hear the're causing trouble."

Bob reached Dayton just before four. The men there had no more information about Indians. Bob galloped on to Reed's, to find there was no relief horse waiting.

"A posse come through and grabbed all the horses so they could chase the Paiutes," the keeper explained.

Bob rested his tired horse, re-saddled, and continued on. When he rode into Buckland's, his relief rider, Johnson Richardson, was too scared to take over. "They killed them all at Hooten Wells," Richardson said through chattering teeth. "Couldn't get a horse there, nohow. They burnt the station to the ground. I ain't riding east into that."

Superintendent W. C. Marley offered Bob an extra fifty dollars if he would make Richardson's ride for him. Although Bob had just ridden seventy-five miles and it was past midnight, he would have to go another 115 to reach the next relief rider.

"I'll leave at once," Bob said.

"There's nothing at Hooten Wells but ashes," Marley said. "I don't know about Carson Sink. Be careful when you ride up."

Bob got a fresh horse at Carson Sink and then rode thirty-five miles without water to Sand Springs. With a fresh horse, he rode on to Cold Springs, reaching that station at noon. On that ride, Bob exchanged shots with a small party of Paiute warriors. The Indians missed him, but put one bullet into his horse. With another fresh horse, Bob rode the last lap to Smith's Creek.

The next relay rider, Jay Kelley, took the mochila and continued east. Pony Bob, exhausted, went to bed. He had ridden 190 miles, stopping only to change horses and eat! It was the fastest ride for that distance in the history of the Pony Express. But Pony Bob was not through!

Nine hours after Bob went to bed at Smith's Creek, the westbound rider galloped in. Bob saddled up, swung the mochila over his saddle, and galloped west. At Cold Springs Bob learned that the Indians had killed the station keeper and stolen all the horses, including the one he had left there on his eastbound ride.

It was getting dark when Bob started for Sand Springs. The road wound through heavy sagebrush, much of it high enough to hide a horse. Bob had learned that his horse's ears were the best danger signal. He watched them carefully. The howling of wolves and yip-yipping of coyotes sent chills down his spine, but he saw no sign of Indians.

Bob reached Sand Springs safely and persuaded Montgomery Maze, the keeper there, to leave the station and ride with him to the Carson Sink. There they found fifteen well-armed men who had been chasing Indians. Bob rested an hour until dark and then rode on to Buckland's.

"They killed the keeper at Cold Springs," Bob told Superintendent Marley, who was still at Buckland's.

When Marley learned that Bob had got the mail through to the next relay rider, he raised the fifty dollar bonus to a hundred. Bob, exhausted again, said the excitement had braced him for the rest of his ride. After an hour and a half rest, he rode on west. When he reached Friday's Station he had ridden 380 miles and was within a few hours of being on schedule.

Suggested reading: W. L. Visscher, A Thrilling and Truthful History of the Pony Express (Chicago: Charles Powner, 1946).

YOUNGEST PONY EXPRESS RIDER

Bill Cody, fourteen, was the youngest Pony Express rider, but he knew how to ride. He had hired on with Russell, Majors and Waddell three years before, when his father died. The company used him to carry messages between their freight outfits. Then, when the firm started the Pony Express, Bill got a short, 45-mile run west from Julesburg.

"But, I want to be in the mountains," Bill said.

The next year — 1861 — he reported to Division Manager Jack Slade, west of Fort Laramie.

"You're too young," Slade said.

"I rode last year out of Julesburg."

"Are you that fourteen-year-old kid — the youngest rider on the line?"

"I'm fifteen now."

Slade assigned Bill a desolate, 76-mile route from Three Crossings on the Sweetwater to Red Butte on the North Platte. It passed Independence Rock, famous landmark for emigrants. From there west the route followed the narrow canyon of the Sweetwater, past the Split Rock and Rock Creek stations. Hostile Sioux and Cheyenne Indians watched the trail carefully, resenting the white invasion of their treasured hunting grounds.

"Watch out for your scalp," Slade warned.

Years later, after Cody had earned his nickname killing buffaloes, he became famous for killing Yellow Hair in one of the West's most celebrated two-man fights. But even at age fifteen, he had no love for Indians. He had killed his first at age eleven.

One day Bill rode into his home station and learned that the rider who was to carry the mail on west had been killed.

"Can you take the next run, too, Bill?" the station keeper asked. "We don't have anyone else for relief."

"Sure," Bill said.

"Had reports of injuns. Keep your eyes peeled."

Bill rode another eighty-five miles, ending at the Rocky Ridge Station. Then he turned around and returned to Red Butte. He had ridden 322 miles, the longest continuous Pony Express ride ever made. Averaging fifteen miles an hour, he had exhausted twenty horses.

A week later Bill was attacked by Sioux, which led to another notable ride. Fourteen warriors jumped him in a sandy ravine, nine miles west of Horse Creek Station. Fortunately Bill was on the fastest and strongest horse the company owned. He flattened himself on the animal's back and dug in his spurs. Arrows whistled past as his roan racer galloped away.

When Bill reached Sweetwater Bridge, he learned that other Indians had attacked there, killing the stock tender, and driving off all the horses. Unable to get a remount, he hurried on to Ploutz's Station. He had galloped the same horse for twenty-four miles!

Later that year Indians attacked a stagecoach just east of Bill's home station, killing the driver and two passengers. They kept stealing horses from all the stations. To ride Bill's route was to run a gauntlet.

Finally the company stopped the express completely for a few weeks. During that time a party of forty stage drivers, express riders, stock tenders, and ranchmen, led by Wild Bill Hickok, rode north to look for Indians with stolen horses. The well armed, well mounted men had all braved every kind of danger and were anxious to tangle with the Indians. Young Bill Cody rode beside Hickok, at the head of the posse.

"Think we'll catch up with them?" Cody asked.

"We'll find them. We got some good trackers."

They found the Indians on Clear Creek, a tributary of the Powder River. Although outnumbered three to one, the posse recovered all the stolen horses, plus a hundred Indian horses.

The celebration lasted three days. Indian horses changed hands with every deal of the cards. On the third night, a stage driver tried to pull an ace from his sleeve. Jack Slade shot him dead, and the posse sobered up quickly.

The Pony Express resumed running. Slade made Cody a special rider, working as a trouble shooter out of Slade's headquarters at Horseshoe Springs. The new job, while dangerous, gave Bill more time for hunting.

Later that summer Bill Cody, a bored fifteen-year-old, quit the Pony Express to join a scouting venture for the Union Army in Kansas. In his own words, he had met with no further "adventure worthy of being recorded."

Suggested reading: Elizabeth J. Leonard & Julia Cody Goodman, *Buffalo Bill: King of the Old West* (New York: Library Publ. 1955).

LIVING MONUMENT

Young Emmet McCain waited at Fort Churchill for the eastbound Pony Express rider. It was spring 1861. A year had passed since the Paiute uprising, but recent reports said the Indians were again attacking up north along the Humboldt River.

"Got government papers in the mail this time, Emmet," the station keeper said. "May be the most important mail you've carried so far. Don't let anything happen to it."

The boy nodded his head and slapped his leg with the green, cottonwood stick that he carried for a quirt. His taut facial muscles revealed his determination.

The hostler brought out the strongest horse at the station, not the fastest one. The animal was saddled and ready to go.

"How come?" asked Emmet. "Won't I need all the speed we got if I run into them redskin devils?"

"If they're on the prod down here, you're likely to find them around Carson Sink," the keeper said. "So I want you to circle north, miss the Sink, and ride straight through to Sand Springs. You'll need endurance more than speed to get the longer ride out of your horse."

"Well, I guess — "

The eastbound rider galloped in and slid to a stop in a great cloud of dust. The hostler jerked the mochila from the horse and slapped it on to Emmet's mount. Emmet leaped into the saddle and galloped away.

"Take it easy with that horse," the hostler shouted. "He's got twice as far to go as usual."

Emmet pounded down the alkali-covered trail and gradually pulled back on the reins until he had his horse in a smooth, ground-eating lope. An hour later, about when he had planned to swing north from the trail to clear the Sink Station by at least five miles, he saw sagebrush smoke rising above some hills ahead. Indians! Signalling his approach!

He swung to his left, leaving the trail. He touched his horse lightly with the cottonwood stick quirt, and the fine animal responded with a faster lope. Soon the warning smoke was behind. Then, as the horse's hooves beat their steady rhythm in the soft ground, Emmet saw movement on a hill ahead. Squinting, he could make out several Paiutes, mounted, armed, and ready for war! They started down a long slope that would intersect Emmet's path.

The boy knew he was trapped. Surely the Indians behind would be riding up to cut off any retreat. Emmet's first thought was of his precious mail. The most important mail I've carried, the keeper had said! I've got to protect it and not let the devils get it!

He touched his horse again with the quirt, and he could feel the muscles working against his legs as the animal galloped faster. Then the muffled drumming sound of the hooves changed, and Emmet knew that he was crossing softer, damper ground. He brought the horse to a quick halt, jumped down, and pulled off the mochila. He pushed a rock to one side and dug out a space in the soft, mushy earth large enough to bury the mochila and its mail.

Then Emmet led his horse back and forth over the disturbed earth until no one could see what had been done. He shoved his green cottonwood quirt into the earth. It would be a marker so he could find the mail if he got away from the Indians. If he did not, maybe someone from the station would recognize it and figure out what he had done. Then Emmet leaped into the saddle, checked his revolver, and galloped away from the approaching Indians.

The two war parties caught him between them. The fight was brief, furious, and hopeless. The warriors Emmet hit were replaced by others. Soon the boy and his horse went down, heroes of the legendary pony mail.

The cottonwood stick sprouted in the moist soil. It became a magnificent, lone tree, about five miles north of the old Pony Express trail. For years it provided cool shade for weary travelers.

When Churchill County, Nevada, was formed, the area containing the tree was named the Lone Tree District. The tree stood many years as a fitting monument to the courage and devotion of Emmet McCain.

C. E. Bartlett bought the property in 1907 and built his ranch house under the tall cottonwood tree, by then almost fifty years old. Twenty-five years later, his widow had to cut down the dead tree as it had become a hazard to her house. It took three tractors, hitched together, to pull out the roots.

Suggested reading: *Pioneer Nevada* (Reno: Harold's Club, 1956).

MUGGINS

Not every one could send mail on the Pony Express. At five dollars a half ounce, even tissue paper made the mail expensive. So mules carried the mail along the same route the Pony riders used, but at a much slower pace. The Pony riders changed horses every twelve to fifteen miles. The mule riders used the same animals every day, riding one and leading two or three pack mules behind.

Bill Streeper had carried mule mail for Chorpenning and Egan over a hundred-mile distance in eastern Nevada for two years before the Pony Express started. Then he continued to carry the slower mail, but was sometimes called as a reserve rider for the express.

Streeper had come west in 1847 as a small boy. He first learned about mules when he freighted down the Old Southwest Trail from Salt Lake City to Los Angeles.

"Mules is jist as smart as horses is," he often said. "You jist gotta understand their language."

Streeper's favorite mule, Muggins, could smell Indians like a pointer smelling grouse. Her talents came in handy during the Gosiute outbreak in 1861.

As Streeper rode west one morning from the Mountain Springs Pony Express Station in eastern Nevada that year, he got his warning from Si McCandless.

"I don't like the goin's on of some of the Injuns around here," McCandless said. "I ain't looking for any perticaler trouble at this station, but a lone man out on the trail orter keep his eyes peeled."

McCandless, who ran a small trader's store across the road from the station, lived with a Gosiute woman and knew many of her relatives. His warning was worth heeding.

"I'll watch keerful," Streeper said. "Take some doin' fer the red devils to slip up on ole Muggins."

A few hours after Streeper left, Gosiutes did attack at Mountain Springs. Two white men were killed and two others ran to the next station east in one of the West's most interesting foot races.

As Streeper approached the Ruby Valley Station, he grew wary, even though unaware of the attack behind him. The Ruby Valley station was hidden from view by big rocks and brush and a turn in the road.

"I rode up pretty cautious," he told Howard Driggs about sixty years later. They sat in Streeper's home just north of Salt Lake City. The 86-year-old man's eyes were clear and his hand steady. He had been reading a magazine without glasses and watching his granddaughter when Driggs drove up.

"I was riding old Muggins, and her ears begun to twitch. I could see something didn't smell jist right to the old lady, so I was extry careful, you bet. Purty soon the pack mules was a twitching their ears, too. You know, in those days I could read a mule's ears better than you can read the dials on these danged automobiles they got now."

The Ruby Valley Station had been burned to the ground. A few embers glowed in the ashes, but not a person or animal could be seen.

"I got out of there as fast as old Muggins could run," Streeper told Driggs. "We never did find the keeper. Lord knows what the redskins done with him."

Streeper soon met the Pony Express rider coming east. When he told the rider about the destruction of the Ruby Valley Station, the rider said he was turning back. Streeper offered to turn around and carry the express mail if the Pony rider would take care of his mule mail. The rider refused, so they both continued west.

When Streeper reached his home station at Roberts Creek, he found two boys, waiting to go east. So he turned around and carried the express mail, in the company of the two boys.

"I ain't responsible for your scalps," Streeper said. "We all better keep a sharp lookout."

When they reached Mountain Springs Station, they found that station's keeper, murdered and scalped.

"What are we gonna do, Bill?" one of the boys asked.

"Get the hell out of here, fast as we can."

They soon reached a fork where the main trail followed the toe of a slope and a cut off went straight ahead. Streeper slacked the reins on Muggins's neck, and the mule chose the main trail.

"It was good mule sense," Streeper told Driggs. "When we got around the point, we saw the Injuns up there on the cut off, a waiting fer us. They had that squaw belonged to Si McCandless with them."

The three riders reached the next station safely. Streeper fed extra hay to Muggins and brushed her carefully as they waited for soldiers to come and re-open the mail line.

Suggested reading: Howard Driggs, *The Pony Express Goes Through* (New York: J. P. Lippincott, 1963).

A GOOD MAN AND A GOOD HORSE

John (Portugee) Phillips partnered with Jim Wheatley and Isaac Fisher as scouts and teamsters on the Bozeman Trail. In fall 1866 they hired on at Fort Phil Kearny, Wyoming, newly built for additional trail protection. Portugee built a cabin for his wife and two children and went to work. Small and wiry, but well muscled, Portugee was quiet and soft spoken. Popular with the army and other civilians, he was a good man with a horse.

On December 21 Captain William Fetterman led seventy-eight soldiers and two civilians out of the fort to rescue a wood train under attack by Red Cloud's Sioux. Fetterman's command, including Wheatley and Fisher, was wiped out. The fort commander, Col. Henry B. Carrington, called for volunteers to ride for help.

Fifteen hundred Indians had the fort surrounded. The closest telegraph — at Horseshoe Station — was two hundred miles away. The temperature had dropped to forty degrees below zero. Soldiers shoveled snow away from the eight-foot-high stockade so Indians could not attack over the top. Portugee Phillips stepped forward, the only one to respond.

"I'll go, Colonel," he said. "I'd like to have your horse and a saddlebag full of biscuits." Carrington's Kentucky Thoroughbred, Grey Eagle, the best horse in the fort, was reputed to be one of the best in the West.

"You may have my mount and anything else you need, Phillips," the colonel said. He called one of the women out of the magazine, where he had sent them with instructions about firing the powder if the Indians overran the fort. He asked her to bake fresh biscuits, while he groomed and saddled his horse. At midnight Phillips slipped out a side gate and disappeared into the howling blizzard.

He knew the Indians would be watching the trail, so he rode parallel with it, but two or three miles away. Grey Eagle, new to the West, could not tell a deep snowdrift from a snow-covered rise in the ground, so Portugee had to rein him constantly. Both the rider and the horse wanted to move fast in the bitter cold, but Portugee knew the danger of a crippling fall. He kept the big chestnut reined in. He did let him run on level stretches of ground.

At dawn, Portugee hid in a brush-filled gulch. He pulled off the wet saddle blanket and rubbed Grey Eagle dry. He fed the horse some grain and ate some of the biscuits. He heated coffee for himself and melted snow so the horse could drink. He covered the horse with his own blanket and they spent the day there, moving around as much as they could to keep their blood circulating in the bitter cold. Portugee knew he dared not fall asleep.

At dusk the wind died down, but the bitter cold hung on. A small party of Indians discovered them and attacked. With bullets flying around them, Grey Eagle carried Portugee to safety, and they moved on through the night. Phillips rode all the next day, that night, and the next day. He marveled at the strength of the colonel's horse. Never had he ridden such a fine animal!

Late on Christmas eve, Indians attacked again. As before, Grey Eagle outran the attackers. But this time, the horse stumbled to his knees a few times during the night's ride.

They reached Horseshoe Station at ten o'clock on Christmas morning. The telegraph operator could not get a message through to Fort Laramie, forty miles away. Portugee climbed back into the saddle and asked Grey Eagle to keep going.

At eleven o'clock on Christmas night, a ghostly apparition slowly approached the Fort Laramie sentry. The soldier opened the gate and watched the strange figure, shrouded with ice and snow, separate into a man and a horse. The man staggered forward, mumbling something about a message. The sentry helped him into Old Bedlam, the fort's entertainment hall, where the officers and their ladies were dancing.

The cold blast of snow and the sentry's shout brought the dance to a halt. Portugee pointed to a pocket inside his buffalo overcoat and then collapsed. His coma lasted many hours. He suffered for weeks from exhaustion and frostbite. He never fully recovered his health. Later he would know that he had made the greatest ride in the history of the West, 236 miles in the coldest winter in fifty years.

Grey Eagle would never know. When Portugee slid off his back, the gallant animal slumped down in the snow and died.

Suggested reading: Jack Schaefer, *Heroes Without Glory* (Boston: Houghton Mifflin, 1965).

BLACKIE

In October, 1870, Lieutenant William F. Butler rode out of Fort Garry on Blackie, a small, black, Canadian pony. The Canadian government wanted Butler to explore the Saskatchewan River valley from Lake Winnipeg to the Rocky Mountains. He set out with Blackie, four other horses, and a Red River cart. His only traveling companions were a Hudson's Bay official in a wagon and a half-Indian helper to drive the cart.

Nights of sharp frost followed cold, sunny days as they moved northwest up the Assiniboine River. On October 30 they crossed the Assiniboine and struck on west, toward the Saskatchewan. Swift-moving masses of ice grated against the necks and shoulders of their horses as they forded the stream.

Butler's horses soon showed the effects of the hard travel, seldom less than fifty miles a day. The cart horses took daily turns in teams of two. Butler was amazed the horses could keep going on the food available. They had nothing to eat but dry prairie grass and no time to eat that except during the cold nights.

Butler was particularly impressed with Blackie, his saddle mount. Day after day the little horse grew more weary, and Butler was sure he would soon give out. Although his black coat grew rough and his flanks lean, the little animal went on "as gamely and pluckily as ever."

Sometimes Butler would dismount and lead Blackie to give him a rest. Then the cart and the wagon would move on, far ahead. If they disappeared over some distant ridge, Blackie would whinny and fret until Butler got back in the saddle and let him trot to catch up. The first job when making camp at night was looking after the horses. Butler would remove Blackie's saddle and rub him down. Then the game little animal would start grazing under the dark sky. Before the men ate their own supper they would lead the horses to a nearby lake or stream, chop holes in the ice, and let them drink.

Sometimes, as he sat by the campfire, Butler would swear to ride another horse and give Blackie a rest the next day. But every morning Blackie looked so fresh and carried his head so high Butler would slip the saddle back on him again. Another day's companionship and talk cemented still further their friendship. Butler said all the little animal asked in return for his hard day's work was for Butler to cut a water-hole in some frozen lake so he could drink at night.

On November 7, after a camp in below-zero weather, they

reached the South Saskatchewan. Masses of ice stretched far out into the river, but in the center a swift, black-looking current filled them with dismay. They had counted on the river being frozen solid.

They made a raft by lashing a tarpaulin around the wagon box. They tried the rest of that day and all the next to get the raft through the ice and across the open water so it could be used as a ferry. They failed, almost drowning in the attempt.

The second night at the river was bitterly cold. By morning the river was frozen solid. They tested the new ice with their axes and decided to try getting their horses across. The lightest one got over all right. The thin ice bent downward in the center, but did not break.

Blackie was next. Two men led him with long ropes. Butler followed close behind to force him forward, if necessary. Again the ice bent downward. But this time, to Butler's horror, it suddenly broke, and Blackie plunged into an icy chasm. Butler jumped back quickly enough to save his own life. The gallant horse kept his head above water as he swam furiously, trying to climb over the crumbling edges of his icy grave.

"Is there nothing we can do?" Butler screamed to the other men.

"Nothing at all," they shouted back. "He's a goner."

Butler watched as the "dumb animal turned to him as one who should help and spoke with un-utterable eloquence from his own agony."

Butler ran back to camp, grabbed his rifle, and returned to Blackie. The horse looked imploringly at him as Butler raised the weapon. His hands shook and trembled. He fired once, and Blackie collapsed, disappearing under the "cold, unpitying ice."

Butler returned to camp, sat down in the snow, and cried like a child.

Suggested reading: William Francis Butler, *The Great Lone Land* (Rutland, Vermont: Charles E. Tuttle, 1968).

OLD FRIEND

Eight-year-old Chester Evans got the new colt in 1874. Chester and his father had moved into a boarding house after his mother died. Busy running his Iowa printing office, the father thought the strawberry roan would be good company for his young son.

When Prince was four and Chester twelve, his father let the boy ride to the Smoky Hill Cattle Pool in Kansas, where an uncle worked.

Too young to work for the pool, Chester did get to ride to Fort Monument and report that the valley was full of hostile Cheyennes, trying to get back to their Dakota homeland. During the eighteen-mile dash to the fort, Chester was hit with five arrows and Prince with one. Chester pulled an arrow out of his shoulder and the shaft of another out of his arm. A sergeant at the fort removed the other four. The wild dash and the arrow in his rump left Prince with a lifetime dislike of Indians.

In 1881 Prince slipped on wet grass and broke Chester's leg as he fell. It took a long time, a lot of pain, and help from Prince to climb back into the saddle. Prince carried Chester nine miles to the ranch. Only the hired girl was home. Chester laid on the floor, his good leg braced against a door jamb. They looped the bridle reins around his other foot.

"Now, rear back against the reins as hard as you can," Chester said, wincing from the pain.

After several tries and much twisting and pulling, the broken leg slipped into place. The girl rode Prince forty-nine miles to the nearest doctor. All the doctor had to do was apply some splints. The leg healed fine.

In January, 1887, the middle of the worst winter in the old West, Chester's uncle told him to ride for a doctor. The young man's aunt was about to have a baby.

"Let Prince rest before you start back," the uncle cautioned.

Chester delivered the message to the doctor in Wakeeney, and put Prince in the livery stable for four hours. They started back at dusk, wind-driven sleet stabbing into them like sharp needles. They traveled all night. At dawn, Chester had no idea where they were. During the next day, Chester fought the numbness in his feet by walking from time to time. He found no shelter — just cold white plains of snow and ice, no canyons, no breaks. Darkness came early.

Several times during the night, Chester would try to sit down and rest. Each time Prince nuzzled him and pawed him gently to keep him moving. On the morning of the second day, Prince stopped at a ranch far to the south of Chester's uncle's place. Thirty-eight men died in western Kansas during that blizzard.

The winter put the uncle out of a job. The Smoky Hill Pool had lost ninety-seven percent of its cattle. Chester moved to Lebo, Kansas, and got married.

Two years later he rode Prince in the race for land, when the Cherokee Strip was opened for settlement. He lived on his claim two years and then moved to California. Before long he and his family — which, of course, included Prince — were back in Lebo for good.

"I bought a little pasture," Chester told J. Frank Dobie in 1940, when he was seventy-eight. "I built a shelter on it for my friend. He would bring in the milk cows in the evening. I would hitch him up to the spring wagon and send him, alone, to the feed store. They knew what to load up, and Prince would always bring it back. My children and all their friends learned to ride on him. He enjoyed his pasture and being with me, especially when I talked to him about the old times."

One day in 1912, when Prince was thirty-eight, the roof of the shed fell in on him. A telephone lineman hurried to Chester's office and told him the horse was trapped.

"We got back as fast as we could run," Chester told Dobie. "He was trapped under heavy timbers, lying across his back. He got him free, but he couldn't get up. We got a board under him and pried him up. I helped him to the spring, where he had a drink. Then he laid down on a nice bed of bluegrass. I stayed with him the rest of that day and all night. Two or three times he lipped my hand like he used to do on the range. I guess he was remembering the old times. The next morning I went to breakfast. When I came back, my friend was dead. No man ever had a better companion or friend."

Suggested reading: J. Frank Dobie, "A Boy and His Horse," in Esquire, September, 1945.

A FAST RIDE TO RESCUE A FRIEND

When Billy the Kid was dealing monte at Fort Bowie, Arizona, he killed a soldier and fled to Sonora. There he became friends with another young gambler, Melquiadez Segura. When Billy killed another monte dealer in Sonora, Segura helped arrange for his escape and fled with him.

The two young gamblers went to Chihuahua City, but they did not get along well with the gamblers there. Right after they left that city, three gamblers who had had disputes with them complained of being robbed and another had disappeared, never to be seen again.

Billy and Segura rode to the Rio Grande and parted company for a while. For the next few months, Billy followed his life of crime on the American side of the border. Then, in fall 1876, about the time of his seventeenth birthday, Billy got word that Segura needed him.

Segura had been arrested and jailed in San Elizario, Texas, about twenty-five miles from Franklin (now El Paso). He hired a Mexican boy to look for Billy, knowing that his best chance for escape lay with Billy's courage and skill.

The Mexican boy found Billy six miles north of Mesilla, about opposite Doña Ana.

"You wait here," Billy told the Mexican boy. "Segura and I'll be on our way back by midnight."

"Señor, no es posible. Eet ees a long way — maybe even ochenta mile." The boy shook his head.

Actually, it was one more than eighty by the most direct route, and Billy probably did not follow the most direct route the whole ride. He had recently obtained a tall, gray horse, a good runner, and he felt confident that he could reach his friend by midnight, even though it was already six o'clock.

"If I know horses, this fellow will make it," Billy said. He patted the gray's neck and sped away.

He rode down the west bank of the Rio Grande between the river and Mesilla, fording at Chamberino. After a thirty-minute battle with rough water, the gray pulled up on the bank, five hundred yards below where they had entered. They rushed on, past Cottonwood's, past Hart's Mills, and on to Franklin, where Billy reined up in front of Ben McDowell's saloon.

It was ten-fifteen, and the gray had covered fifty-six miles at an incredible pace. Billy swallowed a glass of whiskey, fed the gray a handful of crackers, and was back in the saddle within ten minutes. It was almost ten-thirty, and he still had twenty-five miles to go.

A few minutes after twelve, the guard at the San Elizario jail heard a loud knocking at the door.

"Who is it?" he asked.

"Open up," Billy said. "We have two American prisoners."

The guard opened the door to face a drawn pistol.

"Try anything funny and it's your funeral," Billy said. "Just hand over your guns."

The guard and the jailer both obeyed Billy.

"Now let Segura out of his irons."

Billy and Segura shackled the guard and jailer together, gagged them, and fastened them to a post. Billy put Segura on the gray and swam alongside, as they forded the Rio Grande. Within an hour they were sleeping soundly at the ranch of a Mexican friend.

Their friend rode back to San Elizario to enjoy the surprise when the town learned that its prisoner had escaped. He returned before daylight to saddle a fresh horse for Segura. Billy's gray seemed fresh after its short night's rest.

Two hours later a thirty-man armed posse rode up to the ranch. Billy's friend complained about the robber and the escaped prisoner who had stolen his best horse, insulted his wife, and ransacked his house for plunder. He put the posse on the trail, knowing they could never catch his friends. Then he mourned the wickedness of the world, as he counted the coins Billy had left,and watched the posse ride away.

By noon Billy and Segura were back with the messenger, where Billy had started his incredible ride to rescue his friend.

Suggested reading: Pat F. Garrett, *The Authentic Life of Billy the Kid* (New York: Indian Head Books, 1994).

COMANCHE

Captain Tom Custer of the 7th Cavalry drove a choice lot of horses from Fort Leavenworth, Kansas, to Fort Ellis in May, 1868. The quartermaster in St. Louis had bought them from Clem Bates, a rancher in Indian Territory. Bates kept a Kentucky thoroughbred stallion with his mustang and mixed-blood mares, and the government had paid ninety dollars each for the animals. The forty-one horses included a six-year-old bay gelding, weighing a thousand pounds and standing sixty inches high at the withers. He combined the muscular strength and hardihood of his dam with the refinment and endurance of his sire.

Myles Keogh, I Company captain, needed another horse to replace one he had just sold. Officers not only had the first pick of new horses, but, if they chose, they could buy and own a horse as a personal mount. Keogh paid the ninety dollars to the government and stabled the new bay next to Paddy, his other mount. Paddy remained a government horse.

Keogh, an Irish-born veteran of the Papal War and the Civil War, was a dashing cavalryman. Decorated for bravery by both the Pope and the president, he had had horses killed under him in the Civil War and the Indian Wars.

Four months later, on September 14, the new horse got his first wound and his name. In a skirmish with Cheyennes, Arapahoes, and Kiowas south of the Cimarron, he was shot in the right hind quarter. Some say Keogh selected the name because the cavalry mistakenly thought they were fighting Comanches; others say it was because he screamed like a Comanche when Keogh dug the arrowhead out. Whatever the reason, Keogh had named what would become one of the most famous cavalry horses in history.

On June 9, 1870, Comanche got his second wound, an arrow in the right foreleg in another skirmish with Indians. His third wound came from a bullet in the right shoulder on January 28, 1873, as the 7th Cavalry was fighting moonshiners and the Ku Klux Klan in the south. The regiment moved to Dakota Territory later in 1873.

Shortly after noon on Sunday, June 25, 1876, George Custer, field commander of the 7th, halted the regiment as it rode down a creek into the valley of the Little Bighorn in Montana Territory. He divided the regiment into four parts. The five companies staying with Custer were again divided into two battalions. One battalion, companies F, I, and L, was assigned to Keogh as battalion commander. At this time, Keogh switched his saddle from Paddy to Comanche. He preferred to ride Comanche into battle, and he kept him as fresh as possible. However, on that blistering hot day, one of the worst of the year, even the unmounted horses following along with the pack train were soaked in sweat.

About four o'clock, a drenching rain poured down on the dust and blood of the battlefield. Every single officer, enlisted man, and civilian assigned to the five companies that stayed with Custer lay dead. Indian accounts of the battle — the most examined, most talked about, and most written about in our nation's history — said Myles Keogh was the bravest man they ever fought. They told how he had wheeled his horse broadside to protect his men and how, when Keogh lay on the ground, dead, he still clung for a time to the reins.

The victorious Indians added many cavalry horses to their herd that day. They did not take Comanche. When other soldiers reached the battlefield on June 28, they found Comanche in the timber along the river bottom. His blood-soaked saddle had twisted under his belly. His broken bridle hung down from his head. He nickered softly when he recognized Lieutenant Henry Nowlan, Keogh's best friend.

Comanche had six wounds, two in the neck, one in a loin, one in a front foot, and a through and through wound entering the right shoulder and coming out in the left chest. Some say the Indians passed the horse up because of his condition; others mention the respect for his fallen rider.

Soldiers carefully washed Comanche's wounds with zinc water and led him almost twenty miles to a steamboat on the Yellowstone. He, along with wounded soldiers, was hauled to Fort Lincoln, near present Mandan, North Dakota.

Henry Nowlan took command of the new I Company. Until the time of his death, Comanche was often called the honorary captain. Almost two years passed before he had recovered enough from his wounds to move without help. Then, in April, 1878, the army issued the following general order:

1. The horse known as "Comanche" being the only living representative of the bloody tragedy of the Little Bighorn, Montana, June 25, 1876, his kind treatment and comfort should be a matter of special pride and solicitude on the part of the 7th Cavalry, to the end that his life may be prolonged to the utmost limit.

2. The commanding officer of "I" Troop will see that a special and comfortable stall is fitted up for Comanche. He will

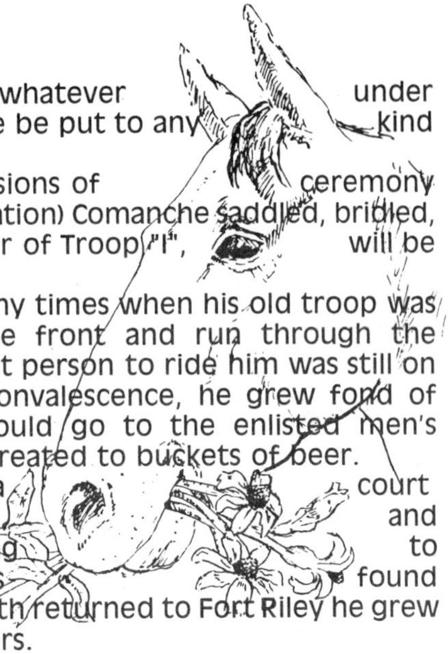

not be ridden by any person whatever under any circumstances, nor will he be put to any kind of work.

3. Hereafter upon all occasions of ceremony (of mounted regimental formation) Comanche saddled, bridled, and led by a mounted trooper of Troop "I", will be paraded with the regiment.

Comanche loved it. Many times when his old troop was drilling he would go to the front and run through the formations, as though the last person to ride him was still on his back. During his long convalescence, he grew fond of whiskey bran mash. He would go to the enlisted men's canteen on paydays and be treated to buckets of beer.

Striking the horse was a court martial offense. Front lawns and flower gardens meant nothing to him. His sign of approval was found in many gardens. When the 7th returned to Fort Riley he grew particularly fond of sunflowers.

Gustav Korn, who was in I Company at the time but missed the Little Bighorn battle when his exhausted horse played out, took charge of Comanche. An often-told cavalry story related that when the 7th was back at Fort Riley, and Comanche could not find Korn on the post, he would trot down the Junction City road to wait in front of a certain woman's house until Korn came out.

The Army's wish that Comanche's life might be "prolonged to the utmost limit" came true. He was six when Keogh bought him, the beginning of a horse's prime period. His age of fourteen at the time Keogh was killed was about the end of that prime of life. Comanche died at twenty-nine on November 6, 1891, equivalent in humans to about a hundred years.

Gustav Korn, Comanche's faithful caretaker for over half his life, was killed at the Battle of Wounded Knee in December, 1890. Perhaps the horse never recovered from his grief.

All of Comanche's body, except the hide, was buried with full military honors. A Kansas University professor preserved the horse through taxidermy. Comanche can be seen today in the Dyche Museum of Natural History at the University in Lawrence.

Suggested reading: Charles L. Convis, *The Honor of Arms* (Tucson: Westernlore Press, 1990).

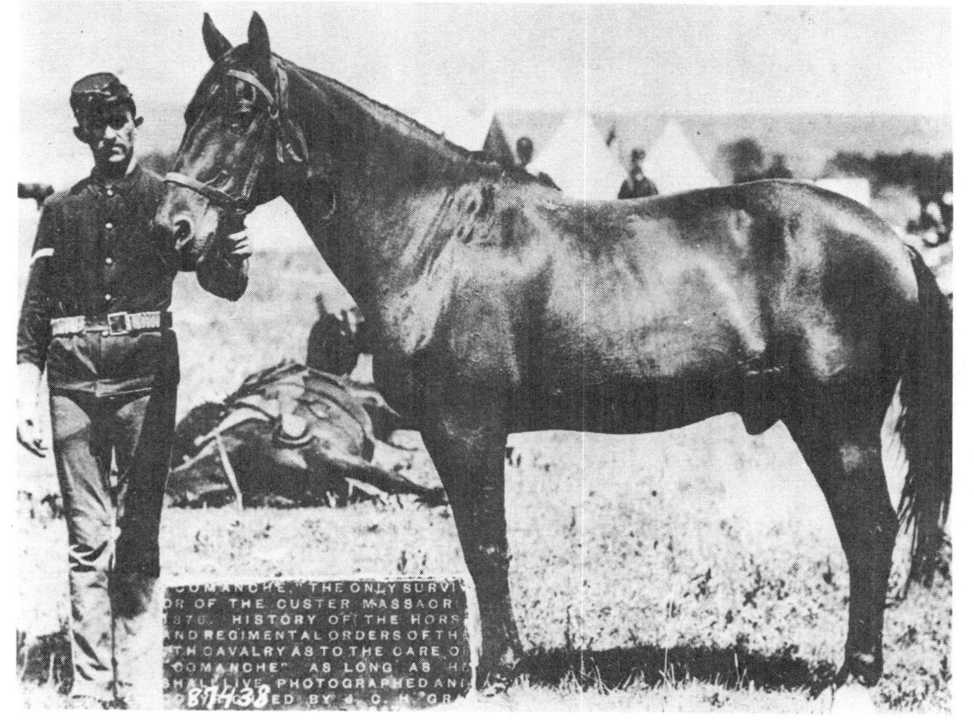

COMANCHE

National Archives

BURIAL OF AN OLD FRIEND

Bill Cheney came to the Yellowstone Valley in 1864 as a wagonmaster with General Sully's expedition. In fall 1877 he was at Fort Buford saddling Nig, his black, half-Morgan horse, for the return to his camp on the river, when the fort commander approached.

"Got dispatches coming from Fort Keogh," the commander said. "Would you keep an eye out for the riders, Bill?"

"Sure will."

As Cheney trotted toward the gate, a buffalo hunter, who had been hanging around the fort for a few days, stopped him.

"Riding out? Guess I'll saddle up and ride with you."

"Come along. Two's better than one with Injuns on the prod."

Hostile Indians had been seen in the valley all summer. Chief Joseph and his Nez Perce were trying to escape to Canada. Cheyennes and Sioux still celebrated their victory over the 7th Cavalry the year before.

"What's your name?" Cheney asked.

"Call me Smith."

Cheney grinned. Many men in the West had only one name. Most were dodging the law or a woman, but it was no one else's business. Cheney was glad to have the company.

They had seen no Indians by the time they reached Cheney's camp, fifteen miles south. Cheney invited Smith to spend the night. They rubbed their horses down and fed and watered them. Then Cheney fixed a supper of antelope steaks and sourdough bread.

"Those riders should be showing up soon," Cheney said the next morning, carrying his saddle to Nig. "I'll ride out a ways with you."

"Like you said, two's better than one."

They rode carefully, watching the valley for Indian sign. After twenty miles they found the bodies of the dispatch riders. Both were freshly scalped, mutilated, and stripped of all possessions.

"My God," each man said in horror, as they stared at the sadistic emasculations.

"Not been dead long," Cheney said. His eyes swept the valley and surrounding hills. He saw Nig's nostrils quivering. "We're about to have company. Look at Nig. He can smell them Injuns."

They heard yells from a clump of cottonwoods.

"Let's get outta here," Cheney said. "Maybe we can outrun them."

A dozen warriors pursued as they galloped away from the river.

"We'll work our way through the hills," Cheney shouted. "Pick off their horses when they get close. They ain't no good on foot."

Smith rode a leggy bay, trained to chase buffalo. While going uphill, they dismounted and ran beside their horses, hanging on to the stirrups. Then they leaped into the saddles and raced the horses downhill. Whenever an Indian got close enough, they would shoot his horse.

After about fifteen miles, they reached the place where Sidney, Montana, is now located.

"We got a good lead, now," Cheney said. "Let's cross the river. I know where there's a good place."

They again heard yells behind as they approached the river.

"Don't stop," Cheney shouted. "We can never make a stand on this side. We got to cross."

He leaned forward, patted Nig's foam-flecked neck, and listened to the rasping breathing sounds. He could feel the heaving ribs between his legs. "Nig," he said "get me out of this scrape and I'll take care of you for the rest of your life."

Nig plunged into the stream, followed by Smith's bay, equally exhausted and trembling. The horses swam across, and Nig struggled up the bank. Smith's bay staggered out and fell dead in his tracks.

Cheney led Nig behind some driftwood and left him there. "Catch your breath boy."

The men crouched behind a log, their rifles trained on the river, waiting. The Indians turned away. A few crossed the river out of rifle range and started in their direction. But after Cheney and Smith both got on Nig and started the fifteen-mile ride to Fort Buford, the Indians chose not to follow.

"You saved my neck, Nig," Cheney said the next morning as he brushed his horse's coat over and over. "And I meant what I said about taking care of you for the rest of your life."

It would be a long life. Nig was six when he saved Cheney. As the years went by, a common sight in the Yellowstone Valley was the faithful horse standing outside a saloon, waiting for his master to come out and go home. Sometimes Cheney would be unsteady on his feet, but Nig was careful to keep him from slipping off as they headed home. As the horse got older, Cheney retired him to his best pasture in summer and to a clean, warm stall in the barn for winter.

Cheney never married. When he got older his niece, Susan Harrison, kept house for him. After Nig had lost all his teeth, Cheney or Susan would cook corn meal mush or oat meal for him. Nig ate whenever he was hungry. He would walk slowly, sometimes unsteadily, from the barn to the kitchen door, and paw the ground until Cheney or Susan came out to feed him. Nig loved alfalfa, but when his teeth were gone, he could not eat the stems. Then Cheney would strip off the leaves, and Nig would gum them down.

One morning in 1912 Andrew Hanto, Cheney's hired man, came to the kitchen and saw the 73-year-old man with his head in his hands.

"What's the matter?" Hanto asked. "Ain't you feeling good?"

Cheney lifted his gray head and looked up with red-rimmed eyes.

"Nig died last night. I found him when I took his breakfast down to the barn." He hesitated. "Son, will you bury him?" His voice trembled.

"Sure," Hanto said. "I'll hitch up the team and drag him out. Where do you want him buried?"

"Just a damn minute." Cheney slowly got to his feet, his old, rheumy eyes blazing, his voice firmer. "You ain't dragging Nig nowhere. You build a stoneboat and we'll roll him over on it. We'll take him out behind the granary and bury him right."

"Yes, sir."

Almost forty-two, Nig was over 120 in equivalent human years. Cheney had Hanto build a coffin out of flooring boards. The hired man dug the grave with a sloping side, so they could slide the coffin into it.

"We ain't dropping him into the ground," Cheney announced. He went to Sidney and bought two of the best blankets he could find. He laid one blanket in the bottom of the coffin, and gently laid the other over Nig, after he had been rolled inside. Hanto struggled with the top of the coffin.

"Close Nig's eyes before you put the lid on," Cheney ordered. "I don't want no dirt sifting into them."

Suggested reading: Kathryn Wright, *Saved by a Horse* (Sidney, Montana: Montana Bank of Sidney, 1969).

BILL CHENEY AND SMITH
ESCAPING INDIANS

STARFACE

They named him for the white, star-shaped patch on his forehead. The ranchers in the far end of what would become the Oklahoma Panhandle saw him many times — fearless, proud-walking, probably mustang and Morgan, the greatest horse thief in this No Man's Land. When his blood stirred he raided the ranch herds, fighting their stallions and adding new bunches of mares to his own well-trained harem. Starface knew all the rough, unfenced country between the Cimarron and Corrumpa Rivers. He knew it all, and he claimed it all.

No one could walk him down; Starface refused to circle. Nor could anyone get close enough to crease him. They could cut off his followers, but the stallion still ran free. Finally, in 1878, the exasperated ranchers had had enough. They picked four cowboys, giving them their strongest and fastest horses.

"Don't come back until you've caught him or killed him."

It took a week of scouting to find the band. For the next three days and nights the cowboys dogged the mustangs, marvelling at their discipline. When Starface left them to graze alone, not a mare followed. Sometimes he rounded them up in a tight band from which no yearling dared break away. Sometimes he led them on a trail, every animal following obediently. He slept less than any animal in his herd.

It was early fall. The moon shone brightly. Shortly after midnight the cowboys on watch saw Starface leave the herd and head for the Cimarron River flats. One followed and the other hurried back to wake their companions. The dew on the grass made trailing easy. Starface galloped north for six miles.

About ten miles east of present Kenton, Oklahoma, the stallion entered a grassy canyon. The rock-walled gorge narrowed into a bluff high above the Cimarron River. The eastern sky was getting light when the cowboys saw Starface's tracks going into the canyon. They knew he would be going back for his mares. They decided to wait for his return. After three days of watching, their vengeance had turned into admiration. They no longer wanted to kill him; just capture him.

In the early light of morning, they saw Starface returning with a dozen mares and colts. The horses were not used to his methods, and he had to run back and forth to force them into the valley. He would check them at one place and whip them up at another until they did as he commanded. Intent on his task like a true craftsman, he was, for once, off guard.

He had worked them into the pass, where the walls were less than a hundred feet apart, before the mares strung out into

a disciplined line. Then suddenly four cowboys galloped out from behind boulders, shooting their pistols in the early morning stillness. The wild Texas yells panicked the mares. Snorting a defiant challenge, Starface darted alone up the steep canyon side.

The cowboys thought he knew a secret way out of the canyon. They watched in awe as he stopped at a break in the wall opposite them. The sunlight glistened on his muscles.

"He's the King of the horse world," one of them said.

Describing the scene afterwards, they all agreed that not one of them would have shot Starface for all the horses north of Red River.

But they soon realized, as Starface knew all along — there was no way out of the canyon. The magnificent animal leaped down to a bench about as large as a big corral. Seamless caprock towered above it. Starface had picked the only place where he could jump down. The other side of the bench loomed ninety feet above the rock-filled bed of the Cimarron.

"Come on, we've got him," yelled one of the cowboys.

"Yeah," shouted another. "There's room to rope him if we're careful and don't fall off. He sure as hell can't get away."

They followed up the wall the way Starface had gone. They saw him racing back and forth along the sheer edge of the bench. As the lead rider dropped down to the bench, Starface made his last dash.

As the stallion reached the brink, he gathered himself as if to vault hundreds of feet across the Cimarron. Without halting a second, he sprang forward, his front feet tucked up, his rear feet extended. For one glorious flash of time he stayed stretched out, his mane and tail streaming, his eyes flashing defiance at the cowboys behind.

They turned their heads in shame when Starface crashed into the rocks far below.

Suggested reading: J. Frank Dobie, *The Mustangs* (Boston: Little Brown and Co., 1952).

A LONG RACE, A SLOW PACE

Jack Best, one of the contestants, told Jack Thorp about a five-hundred mile endurance race in the early 1880s from Deadwood, Dakota Territory, to Omaha:

Flashy speed or tricks would be no 'count. Not like your usual pasture or street race. The time you hit the finish only counted forty percent. The rest depended on the condition of your horse. Every horse had to be a regular cow horse, none over fifteen hands. I guess that was to keep out the thoroughbred racers. Total weight of rider and saddle had to be at least one hundred and ninety pounds.

The prize?

There was four purses. First was a thousand dollars in cash, to be handed over personal by Buffalo Bill. The other three added up to another thousand.

The distance?

They said the closest way was five hundred and thirty miles, but you could pick your own route. Each rider had a helper with a buckboard or hack to bring along food and bedding. We had to ford all creeks and rivers as we come to them.

How many entered?

There was ten at first, but Hank Singleton come out of the corral on a young, bronky horse, leading the one he would ride. The crowd must have scared the young bronk. He got into a pitching storm just before the start — fell on Hank and broke his leg, so there was only nine of us left. But Hank's sister got the judges to let her ride Hank's horse, so there was ten after all, nine men and a girl.

What kind of a horse did you have?

A little dun, branded Diamond A. He come from a ranch down in Deming, New Mexico Territory. He wore a naught-sized shoe and was glass-eyed. He had a black mane and tail and a dark line down his back. He stood fourteen-two. They poked a lot of fun at him, 'cause he was the smallest in the race. But I knew them duns had a lot of bottom, and I'd been exercising him for a month. Started out at ten miles a day with three feeds of oats and got him up to thirty miles a day. His name was Johnnie Dun. He was hard as rocks.

Much money bet on him?

No. The gamblers posted odds of four to one that he wouldn't even finish. You see, we started on a Saturday at six in the morning. To qualify, you had to finish by midnight the next Saturday. There was one old cowhand bet twenty-five dollars on Dunnie. He had ridden him up from New Mexico a couple years

before. The betting favorites were Ranger and Hornet and the horse Singleton's sister rode, Once Again.

What was the start like?

Three took off at a high lope, throwing dust and gravel. Five hit a slow gallop or a trot. Dunnie was straining on the bit, but me and the Singleton girl started out with a flat-footed walk. She went on ahead, but I stuck to the pace and stopped at eleven for a two hour rest. When we crossed Box Elder Creek, I let Dunnie stand in the water and cool his legs. He liked that.

My brother Bill drove our buckboard with a team of mules. He had supper waiting for me. I rode another twelve miles after supper. Then I sponged Dunnie off on his back, legs, and shoulders with alcohol, washed out his nostrils, rubbed him dry, and put a blanket on him. Then I turned in for a good night's sleep.

Bill called me at four. I gave Dunnie a good rubbing to take out the stiffness. I switched to my other Navajo saddle blanket and told Bill to wash the one that was still damp when he come to a creek. I passed six of the other horses that morning. Then, by eleven, all the horses but one had passed me. That was pretty much the way every day went.

When the Singleton girl caught up, she knew her horse wouldn't make it. She told me that about a hundred thousand dollars had been bet on the race. The local money in Deadwood was on Ranger and Hornet and her horse. Most of the money bet in Omaha and Lincoln went on a black named Coaly. Him and Dunnie were the only ones in the race that weren't local around Deadwood. She thought a ring of gamblers had sent Coaly in to win and they'd do anything to see it happen. I told her I'd watch out.

We kept up the same grind. I'd be ahead at night camp. Then they'd all pass me the next morning. Shortly after crossing Pass Creek, the number seven horse galloped by. His rider shouted, "See you in Omaha." In fact, he never got to Omaha.

When we reached the White River, they was all waiting as though they was scared to get wet. Dunnie jumped right in and swam across and all the rest followed.

When we reached Mission, seven of us were all camped

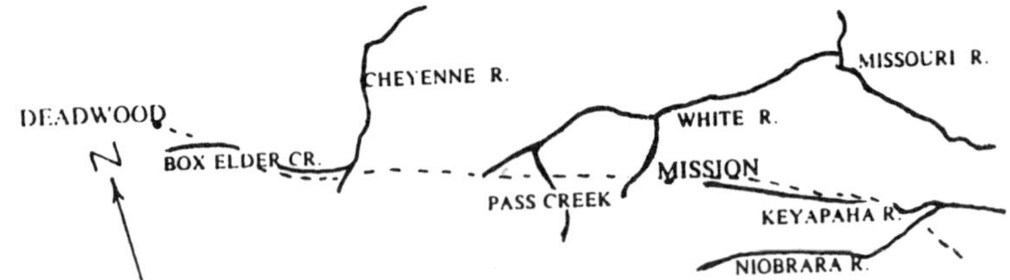

pretty much together. The other three, including the Singleton girl, had dropped out. The next day Bill and I had a nice piece of luck. Shortly after I crossed the Kehapaha River, Bill told me that the regular road we was all following was a muddy quagmire for many miles ahead. We pulled out and rested until all the others had passed. Then we turned off and rode along higher ground. When we hit the Niobrara that evening, I was ahead of everybody. In fact, no one caught up with us until nine the next morning. It was Hornet and Ranger. They was covered with mud, and we learned that two more riders had quit.

The next evening I learned that there was only four horses left, as the other one had quit. I rode ten miles in the dark after supper and Bill said we had gone about three hundred and ten miles. I felt pretty good, since we still had three days to ride.

After we passed O'Neill and were following the Elkhorn River, the other three horses caught up. They all looked pretty tired. As they pulled up to us, Bill said, "Keep your eyeballs oiled, Jack. I hear something's up."

Sure enough, the other riders had a proposition. They said we should divide the cash evenly, no matter who won, and we'd cut the cards to see who would be the first into Omaha. The Hornet rider did most of the talking.

"We'll sort of make a private pool of the money, and our horses can take it easier," he said.

I didn't know what might happen with tens of thousands bet on the others and only twenty-five on Dunnie. Besides, I thought Dunnie was way ahead on his condition. So I said, "It's still a hoss race as far as I'm concerned."

Bill and I decided to keep an extra close watch on Dunnie and to not stop near the others again. A crowd cheered as I rode through Neligh, and an old fellow ran out and handed me a bottle of whiskey. "Go to it, old Diamond A," he shouted. I figgered he had worked some down in New Mexico and knew the brand. When the others came in and camped near us that evening, we kept real quiet.

We had a hell of a surprise the next morning! I got away on Dunnie at four-thirty. The other three were already gone! We only had seventy miles to go, and I kept thinking that they might be ten or twenty miles ahead already. It was hard to keep Dunnie on his

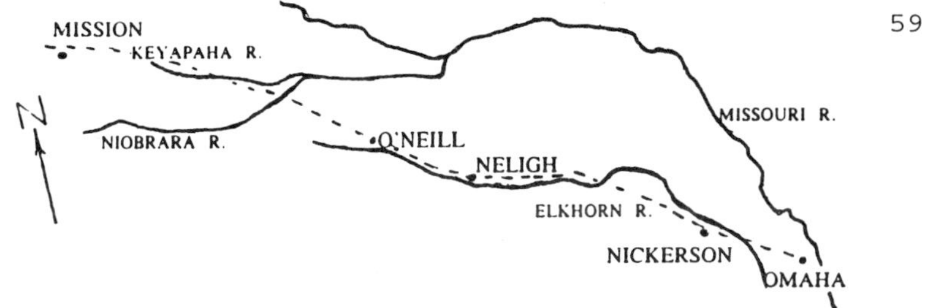

schedule of walk one hour — trot one hour. I knew he was tired, but he still had a lot up his sleeve.

I caught up with Bill at ten-thirty. I had ridden thirty miles and had forty to go. He said the others were only four miles ahead and going pretty slow. I still stopped to rest Dunnie for two hours, but it was hard to do, knowing that the others were getting closer to the finish. Dunnie had lost some flesh over the week, but he didn't look drawn.

We passed though Nickerson about four. I caught up with Bill at six. He had supper ready. He said the other riders were pushing their dead-tired horses for all they were worth. I gave Dunnie his last alcohol rubdown, and we were away at seven.

At ten we passed the three riders and met a dozen of Buffalo Bill's cowboys, who came out to escort us in. I still worried about Coaly, the big, black thoroughbred. I knew Dunnie was in the best condition, but I wanted to be the first across the finish. I knew blood would tell, and even though Coaly seemed to be dead on his feet, I worried that he still had some drive left.

Just inside the city limits, Coaly came pounding up from behind. The town was lighted up like daytime and the sidewalks was crowded with people. Coaly took the lead, and the crowd roared.

"Don't race him," Bill yelled.

Dunnie, being the smaller, seemed to get most of the cheers.

"Come on, you little buckskin."

"Come on, you big black."

The black was a better horse than Dunnie, but he hadn't been as well treated during that long week. I gave Dunnie the spurs for the first time in five hundred miles. We crossed the finish just two lengths ahead!

To this day, I don't know what Buffalo Bill said when he handed me the check, but the check said one thousand dollars.

Suggested reading: Jack Thorp, *Pardner of the Wind* (Caldwell: Caxton Printers, Inc., 1945).

THE GREAT COWBOY RACE

It started as a joke. A reporter on the *Dawes County Journal* at Chadron, Nebraska, who also served as local correspondent for eastern papers, was stuck for a wire story. He cooked up the idea of a cowboy horse race to the 1893 World's Fair, then being held in Chicago. Buffalo Bill Cody, whose Wild West Show was packing them in at the fair, thought it a great idea. He sent this telegram to Dawes County Sheriff, Jim Dahlman:

Am delighted to hear of the proposed thousand-mile race from Chadron to Chicago. Would appreciate having the race end at my Wild West show in the Columbian Exposition. Will donate five hundred dollars to be added to the purse of the winning rider. Colonel (Buffalo Bill) Cody.

How could Chadron citizens back down now? They called a meeting, set up rules, and raised the winner's purse. Each rider would use two horses, riding and leading them alternately. The minimum weight for rider, saddle, and blanket was 150 pounds. Each rider had to check in at points along the course as set by the committee.

Eight riders entered. Best known was Doc Middleton, a local gambler who rode Geronimo and Jimmy. Joe Gillespie entered with Billy Mack and Billy Shafer. At 186 pounds, Gillespie was asking his horses to carry a total of 223 pounds. Jim Stevens, a young cowboy called Rattlesnake Pete, rode up from Kansas to enter. Joe Campbell came all the way from Denver. John Berry, a 38-year-old stage driver, needed the money for his wife and kids. He would ride Sandy and a half-thoroughbred chestnut stallion named Poison. Davy Douglas, Charlie Smith, and Emmet Albright also entered.

The race started at five-thirty in the morning on June 13 in front of the Hotel Blaine in Chadron.

For three days the riders kept close together. Then Davy Douglas dropped out. A day or two later one of Doc Middleton's horses strained a tendon. He said he would stay in as long as the remaining horse could keep up. He and Rattlesnake Pete and Joe Gillespie took turns in the lead.

Doc Middleton, with only the one horse left, was the first to cross the Missouri River and ride through the streets of Sioux City, Iowa. John Berry, riding Sandy the most to keep Poison fresh, was fifth at that point.

Berry moved up steadily and was in the lead when he reached Fort Dodge, Iowa. A four-day rain slowed the riders down. On the tenth day out of Chadron, Berry, just barely ahead of Rattlesnake Pete and Joe Gillespie, reached Waterloo, Iowa.

By now the whole country followed the reports of the race. A Chicago correspondent pedalled a bicycle alongside Berry and his horses. Berry reached Freeport, Illinois, still in the lead with Gillespie close behind. Rattlesnake Pete had finally given up.

At DeKalb, with seventy miles to go, Berry moved his saddle from Sandy to Poison. He left behind the game horse which had borne the brunt of the long ride to keep the thoroughbred fresh for the end. Gillespie rode in an hour after Berry rode out with Poison.

Berry let Poison have his head all through the night. At seven the next morning, they rode through cheering crowds in Chicago suburbs. The crowds increased as they turned south on Michigan Boulevard toward the Wild West show at 65th Street. Buffalo Bill, his cowboys, Indians, and Cossacks all turned out to greet the exhausted man and his gallant horse. At 9:45 Berry slipped down from the saddle.

"Can some of you boys rub him down?" Berry asked. "He damn near ran all night, and I'm all in."

Buffalo Bill's cowboys rubbed the horse with liniment and washed out his nostrils and mouth. Officers from the Humane Society examined Poison and said he was in good shape.

An hour and a quarter later, Emmet Albright rode in to receive a great welcome. His glory was short-lived. The Chicago reporter said Albright had shipped his horse part of the way from DeKalb, so Abright was disqualified.

At one-thirty Joe Gillespie rode in, weighing six pounds less than when he started. A few minutes later, Charlie Smith checked in on Dynamite. The next morning Doc Middleton reported on his lone horse.

Berry got the $1500 first-prize money. Buffalo Bill's five hundred dollars was divided between the other three finishers. The Humane Society gave all the horses a clean bill of health.

The thousand miles had been covered in thirteen days and sixteen hours. Berry and his two horses had averaged seventy-three miles a day for thirteen days in a row.

Suggested reading: Frazier Hunt and Robert Hunt, *Horses and Heroes* (New York: Charles Scribner's Sons, 1949).

ORDERING INFORMATION

True Tales of the Old West is projected for several volumes.

Proposed titles include:

Warriors and Chiefs	In print
Soldiers	In print
Native Women	In print
Mountain Men	In print
Pioneer Women	In print
Ranchers and Cowboys	In print
Horses and Riders	In print
Miners	In Print
Entertainers	In print
Frontiersmen	Soon to appear
Law Enforcers	Soon to appear
Outlaws	Soon to appear
Writers	Under way
Scouts	Under way
Homesteaders	Under way
Dogs and Masters	Under way
Explorers	Under way
Lawyers & Judges	Under way
Railroaders	Started
Merchants	Started
Army Women	Started

Ask at your bookstore or write:

PIONEER PRESS
Box 216
Carson City, NV 89702-0216